NIGHT & DAY

Twenty four hours in the life of Dublin City

Dermot Bolger

and

Przełożyli Justyna
Cathal McCabe
Eileen Casey
Monica Carpenter
Niamh Bagnell
Marie Gahan
Blathnaid Nolan
Brian Kirk
Kate Dempsey
Siobhan Daffy
Adenice Adedoyin
Eva Kelly
Bridget Connors
Tony Higgins
Aine Lyons
Nessa O'Mahony
Padraig J Daly
Colm McGlynn
Áine Ní Ghlinn
Joan Power
Betty Keogh
Gerard Smyth
David Mohan
Kevin Power
Colm Keegan
Maria Wallace
Muireann Allen
Mae Newman

With photographs by
Denis Connolly and Anne Cleary

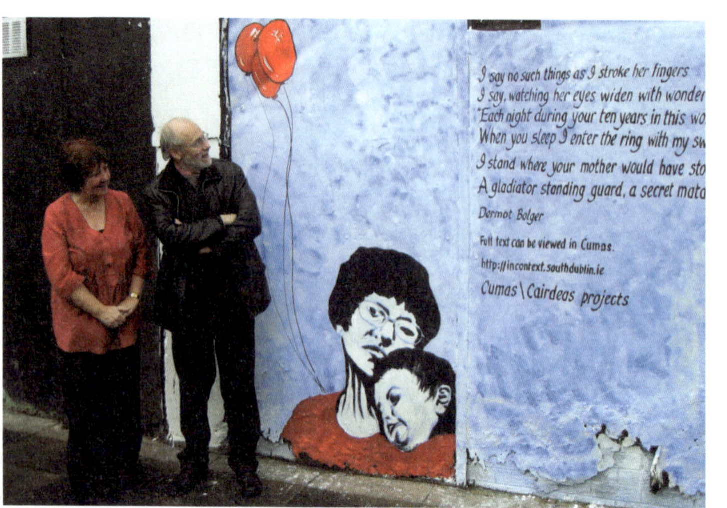

Born in Dublin in 1959, Dermot Bolger's nine novels include ***The Woman's Daughter, The Journey Home, Father's Music, The Valparaiso Voyage*** and most recently ***The Family on Paradise Pier.*** His debut play, ***The Lament for Arthur Cleary***, received The Samuel Beckett Award and the first of his Ballymun Trilogy, ***From These Green Heights***, won the Irish Times/ESB Award for Best New Irish Play of 2004. Author of eight volumes of poetry, he has been Playwright in Association with the Abbey Theatre and Writer Fellow in Trinity College, Dublin. He devised the best-selling collaborative novels, ***Finbar's Hotel*** and ***Ladies Night at Finbar's Hotel*** and has edited many anthologies including ***The Picador Book of Contemporary Irish Fiction.***

As a resident artist in South Dublin County Council's INCONTEXT3 Percent for Art Programme, he wrote ***Walking the Road***, a play which explores the life of the poet Francis Ledwidge and, through him, the forgotten lives of young men from South Dublin County who died in the First World War. Published by New Island Books in association with INCONTEXT3, ***Walking the Road*** has been staged to acclaim in Ireland, Belgium, The USA and Britain.

His poems in this book also form part in a separate solo volume of his recent poetry, ***External Affairs***, published by New Island Books to coincide with ***Night & Day.***

NIGHT & DAY

Twenty four hours in the life of Dublin City

Devised & edited by
Dermot Bolger

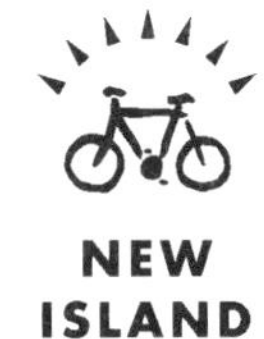

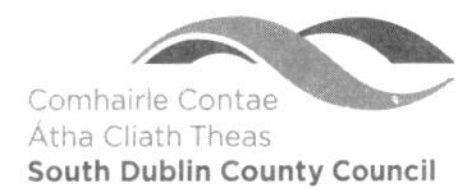

Night & Day

Is first published in Ireland in 2008 by
New Island Books
2 Brookside,
Dundrum Road,
Dublin 14.

In association with
South Dublin County Council

ISBN: 978-1-84840-027-6

British library cataloguing in Publication Data. A CIP catalogue record of this book is available from the British Library.

Designed & typeset by
Yellowstone Communications Design
23 South Great George's Street,
Dublin 2.

New Island received financial assistance from The Arts Council (An Chomhairle Ealaíon), Dublin, Ireland.

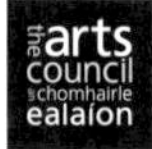

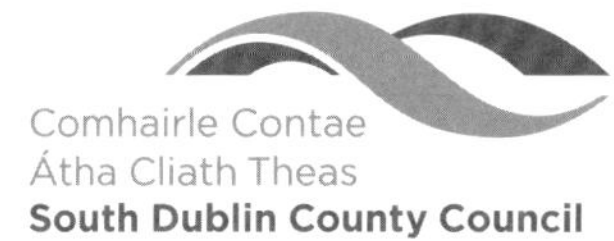

Night & Day by Dermot Bolger was commissioned under South Dublin County Council's INCONTEXT3 Programme which is funded by the Department of Environment Heritage and Local Government and the National Roads Authority.

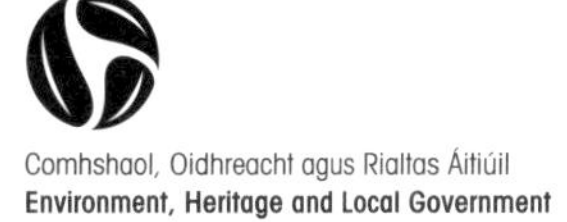

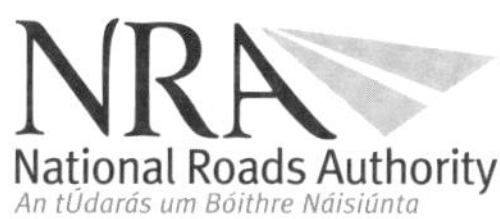

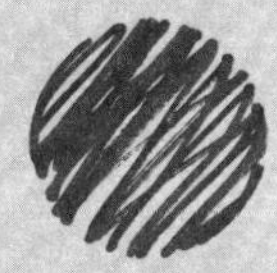

Introduction

Dermot Bolger

As a poet you can witness the start of a poem's journey. This generally begins as a stray thought which sparks with such sudden electricity that you feel you must find a pen and paper and write it down before whatever unexpected magic exists there disappears. This is the stage of a poem's journey that the writer can control. In each successive draft the poem remains a secretive thing, an embryo that you nurture in your mind, working towards the final draft when you risk bringing it out into the light, but always aware that if you procrastinate for too long you risk worrying to death whatever slim magic once existed in the words.

Once asked how he knew that a painting was finished, Picasso replied, "when the gentleman from the gallery comes to hang it." As a playwright I've discovered that a play is only finished when gentlemen and ladies from the press come to hang the playwright. But as a poet you may never know when a poem is truly finished because it rarely enjoys the feedback of a first night or public unveiling. The poems you send out may be pebbles that make a splash somewhere, but the ocean seems so vast that ripples rarely stretch back to you. Sometimes you also may have a sense that the audience that the poem has reached (while welcome, because one feels a sense of privilege if a poem reaches any audience) is not necessarily the intended audience for which it was written.

That is because when you post off your poem to whatever periodical may publish it, you lose control of the process by which it finds its audience. The poem is no longer your secret; it has slipped beyond you into an environment where you have little influence on how or where it may be read.

This has made the writing of my own poems in this book (which comprise roughly half the contents here) so special for me: the fact that I could write them in the knowledge that they would find their first audience by being seen by passers-by in the very specific physical locations that I had written them for public display. The second thing that made them special was the fact that I was not writing them in isolation. These poems were written with the intention of deliberately forming only one half of a story, of being one hand in a collective handclap. I was hoping that my voice would gradually form part of a symphony of other voices; that the lives (whether imagined or recounted) in my poems would merge into a broader tapestry of lives and that this myriad kaleidoscope of voices would hopefully capture some sense of what it feels like to live in South Dublin Country today.

I hoped for this to be achieved through a loose quilt of poems that would form a series of snapshots taken on the run amid the flow of busy lives across Tallaght, Clondalkin, Lucan, Rathfarnham, Templeogue and the old villages becoming new towns in places like Rathcoole and Newcastle. But while it is hoped that this ensemble of voices will form a unique portrait of the part of Dublin which inspired the poems, I feel that, by extension, it reflects something of the wider universal experience of life in any bustling city constantly rewriting its boundaries as it develops.

If I had an ideal reader for this collaborative collection it would be somebody just discovering the possibilities of language for themselves and the freedom which language bestows. Because once anyone begins to write – be it poetry or fiction or song lyrics or simply keeping a diary – this seems to me to be a declaration of independence. In a world which increasing wants you to exist purely as a consumer, it shows that you may be refusing to be seduced by the great lies. Instead you are using words to form your own judgements that may challenge readers and, far more importantly, challenge yourself, as you probe down to the bedrock of the hopes, fears and contradictions that constitutes us all.

These poems are deliberately rooted in one time and place because often when this ideal reader begins to write, they have a sense that literature must have a capital L – that it is probably about lives which occur elsewhere. I know this because I grew up in an environment where I felt that my experiences weren't reflected in literature. Therefore as a writer I've always tried to write in a way that touches upon hidden lives. I began as a teenager by selling photocopied broadsheets of work by local poets in Finglas pubs, hoping to reach a readership who rarely encountered poetry. Now – though Ireland has greatly changed – I have found that in this present project I have echoed that process in some ways by trying to initially display my poems in unexpected locations across South Dublin County where people may rarely encounter poetry.

My poems here were first published as posters or as murals on walls in places as diverse as the Belgard Luas stop in Tallaght or the gable of the Cúnas and Cairdeas Centre in Neilstown – which houses the local Drugs Task Force and where the poem *Neilstown Matadors* is set. It allowed me the rare privilege of being able to sometimes position poems in the very locations that inspired them. I am not naïve enough to imagine that poems by me or by anyone are likely to ever effect a broad constituency when displayed in any public space. But always I was seeking the one person in five hundred who turns a familiar corner and is surprised to see some hint of their own experience reflected back at them from a wall. These posters and murals became my way of leaving the sort of sign which I had longed for as a disaffected youth, a glimpse into another method of seeing things, an affirmation of the validity of thinking in a different way, or – perhaps even better – a sense that the writer has got it wrong and you could find better words to describe what he wanted to capture.

Because wherever these poems first appeared – whether in local parish newsletters, as murals, as posters in public libraries, theatre foyers or motor tax offices, or simply as words and video images projected onto pavements in Tallaght and Clondalkin at night – there was always an invitation for writers who lived or worked in (or felt themselves in some ways part of) the evolving landscape of South Dublin County to join with me on this imaginative journey. I invited them to send me poems that in some way reflected something of their experience of life. The other half of this book consists of a selection of those submissions that brim with a sense of the life experience of their authors and, in one sense, are probably more "true" than mine.

Because my poems here are generally observational and speculative, often deliberately fictional in being written in the voices of others to try and describe a different type of truth. I wanted to strip away the "I" from my poetry and use instead the "eye" through which we perpetually observe fellow commuters, strangers we pass on streets, people with whom we share busy lifts or supermarket check-out queues, the others whose lives we find ourselves unconsciously speculating about. INCONTEXT3 allowed me this time to be an observer, to journey through Clondalkin and Rathfarnham and Tallaght and other places and to imaginatively reinvent the thoughts of a woman I saw waiting for a tram, a foreign worker alighting from one, a teenage girl on a street, a man walking alone at night, a women trapped in the glacier of a bottle-necked motorway, the people we generally pass and forget, people whose lives I suddenly had time to speculate upon or people I met who took the time to talk me about their lives.

Therefore real and reinvented lives jostle throughout these pages, but I wanted this book to be more than just a miscellany of poems. I wanted it to reflect the journey of an ordinary day and one that – unlike most literary journeys – I would not travel alone. A writer's work is essentially solitary, as they try to breathe life into the phantoms of their imaginations and engage in tentative projects that they do not know anyone else will ever read. I therefore found it imaginatively very exciting to know that other people were writing too, about their own lives, that my writing was forming part of a larger project.

My poems were written as a strand of INCONTEXT3, which is South Dublin County Council's Per Cent for Art programme. The premise of this programme was to commission public art of excellence in South Dublin County, to display an on-going commitment to sustainable public art projects in all art disciplines and active engagement with situation, community and place. The commissions allowed artists the time and opportunity to explore new ways of working and allow communities to find new ways of connecting with this work. Inherent to INCONTEXT3 was a marked openness with regard to artistic outcomes; it had an emphasis on slowing the artists time to explore ideas and realise projects within a supportive environment.

After an international open competition several commissions were awarded across various artistic disciplines. Other commissioned artists included Anne Cleary and Denis Connolly, Bik van der Pol, Jackie Sumell and Jenny Walshe. A sculptural commission for the Kingswood Interchange was awarded to Andreas Kopp. These projects were independent of each other, but I am delighted that the opportunity has arisen in this book to collaborate with two remarkable Irish born and Paris based artists, Anne Cleary and Denis Connolly, who have created an extensive archive of images of South Dublin as part of their fascinating and innovative project entitled *City Loops*. The images that accompany my own poems in this book all formed part of original posters designed by Yellowstone Communications of George's Street in Dublin – one of Ireland's most respected design companies. But the images of daily life in South Dublin County that accompany the poems by other writers were taken by Anne Cleary and Denis Connolly during their INCONTEXT3 project and I wish to express my sincere thanks to them for their cooperation, advice and permission to reproduce them here. This strand of photographs by Anne Cleary and Denis Connolly are not intended to directly illustrate the poems, but to provide a visual context for them, a quick moving portrait of the unique place about which they were written.

Public art is not new in Ireland, but it has often been focused on sculpture or other site-specific pieces displayed in an obvious public arena. It is clear to see how a bronze sculpture by the side of a motorway or in a public park relates to that place. Passers-by may love it or disliked it, children may playfully clamber over it or youths choose to vandalise it, but generally there is a sense that it fits naturally into a public space.

Poems, by their nature, can rarely form part of any visual landscape. They are private acts, generally about personal emotions. My challenge with INCONTEXT3 was to create a strand of literature that was both public and private.

I tried to do so in several ways. Firstly by initially publishing the poems in unexpected places, so they formed the pages of a public book left open on gable ends or platforms or projected onto pavements. This allowed the poems to sometimes take on lives of their own, like when a group of students working with a graffiti artist later used one poem to decorate their school library or when a class of mature adults returning to education created their own mural based around the poem *Graffiti on a Corner.*

Secondly, as I have explained, I tried to leave a free space between each of my poems so that people living or working in South Dublin County would not just be the audience but would also become the co-authors of the finished book – that this book would belong to them as much as to me. *Night & Day* therefore displays my South Dublin County poems in the context of the work of fellow writers working around me. A smaller companion volume, *External Affairs* (New Island Books, 2008) displays my two original poems sequences for this project, *County Lives* and *The Clondalkin Suite* (that make up my half of this book) in the different context of the other poetry that I have been writing in recent years.

I would like to thank all the writers who sent me work – those whose work I could use and those whose work, for reasons of space, it was unfortunately impossible to include. It was exhilarating to interact with so many varied voices, many well known to me – like Padraig J Daly and Gerard Smyth, both of whom I have read and admired since I was a boy – and newer voices who are just starting out as writers and who are seeing their work published here for the first time. To all of these colleagues I owe a debt of gratitude and I hope that they have enjoyed the experience as much as I have.

I owe a debt of gratitude to the wonderful support team behind INCONTEXT3, to Rachel McAree, Claire Nidecker, Sarah Searson, Colette Ryan, to Caroline Orr who was there at the start, and to Orla Scannell, South Dublin County Council's Arts Officer, who has been a hugely supportive presence. I would like to thank Leo Duffy, James Keane and all the design team at Yellowstone Communications Design and Edwin Higel and everyone in New Island Books. My thanks to Fiona Ness, Helen Boylan and Nadine O'Regan, who published a selection of these poems as a monthly sequence in the *Sunday Business Post,* after they had firstly being displayed across South Dublin. My thanks to the constantly supportive and friendly staff at all the branches of South Dublin County's Public Library Service where these poems were displayed. Similarly to the staff of the Civic Theatre in Tallaght, the Quarryvale Community and Leisure Centre, the Quarryvale Family Resource Centre, Rowlagh Parish Church, Clondalkin Civic Offices and Motor Tax Office, Tymon Park Visitors Centre, Property Path, the Tallaght Institute of Technology, Collinstown Park Community College, Collinstown Park Sport and Community Centre, Ronanstown Youth Service, Ronanstown CPD, the Get Ahead (After School) Club, Neilstown, the Cumas and Cairdeas Centre, Neilstown and Honeybears Crèche in Quarryvale (who found space for two specially written children's poems not included here). My thanks too to Laura Flynn, Landscape Architect with the Railway Procurement Agency; to the artist Peter Farrell who created a wonderful video projection based on the poem *"Woman Waiting for the Luas",* screened onto the pavement in Clondalkin and Tallaght, to *The North Clondalkin Buzz* (The North Clondalkin Community Development Project newsletter), *The Irish Times* and *The Sunday Independent* who published individual poems after they had first appeared on posters and murals and to the Clondalkin Gazette who distributed *Neilstown Matadors* as a free poster insert.

A very special and sincere thanks to Fiona Delaney, SDCC Arts Development Worker in North Clondalkin who curated the sequence with this book originally called *The Clondalkin Suite,* and who worked so closely with the community in North Clondalkin in selecting the indoor and outdoor locations for these poems. A heartfelt thanks also to John Carpenter, the talented mural artist, who created the wall murals that incorporated many of these poems and who was such a pleasure to work with.

I have not put an overall dedication on this book because I do not own it. But if I could dedicate my selection of poems scattered throughout it, they would be dedicated to my fellow authors who came with me on this journey of trying to produce a series of snapshots of life as lived today in one single part of Ireland. To work with them and watch this book evolve has been a privilege. But in the end every poet must let go of his or her work, let it move out into the wider world and hope that someday a ripple eventually reaches back. Many of the poems assembled here recount diverse everyday journeys. Together they now commence a new journey, all separate pieces of poetry and yet reflecting off one another, complimenting, counterpointing and juxtapositioning, sharing this public space of one single volume, yet continuing to be intensely personal and private experiences. In this way I suppose they are like the busy commuters whose lives they try to capture. May they journey well.

Dermot Bolger,
October, 2008.

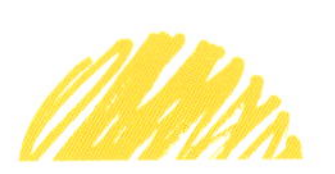
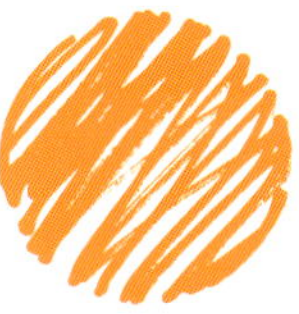
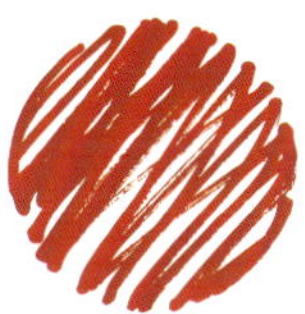
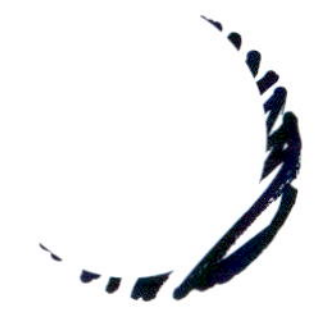

Contents

Contents

Evening

Night

Morning

On the 7am Luas to Tallaght

Dermot Bolger

I never thought that the West would be like this:
Trying to sleep on the tram to Tallaght at dawn,
My mouth so dry I can no longer taste your kiss.

Swapping words in ten languages for tiredness,
Fellow passengers stare out, barely able to yawn:
They never thought the West would be like this.

This journey compounds every ache of loneliness.
I close my eyes, unable to stop thinking of home,
My mouth so dry I can no longer taste your kiss.

Last night on the phone I could sense your stress,
Our children no longer asking when will I come:
I never thought that the West would be like this.

To them I'm now a cheque from a foreign address,
A man who builds apartments we could never own,
My mouth so dry I can no longer taste your kiss.

All day I will shovel cement, yearning to caress
Your neck with each button of your blouse undone:
I never thought that the West would be like this,
My mouth so dry I can no longer taste your kiss.

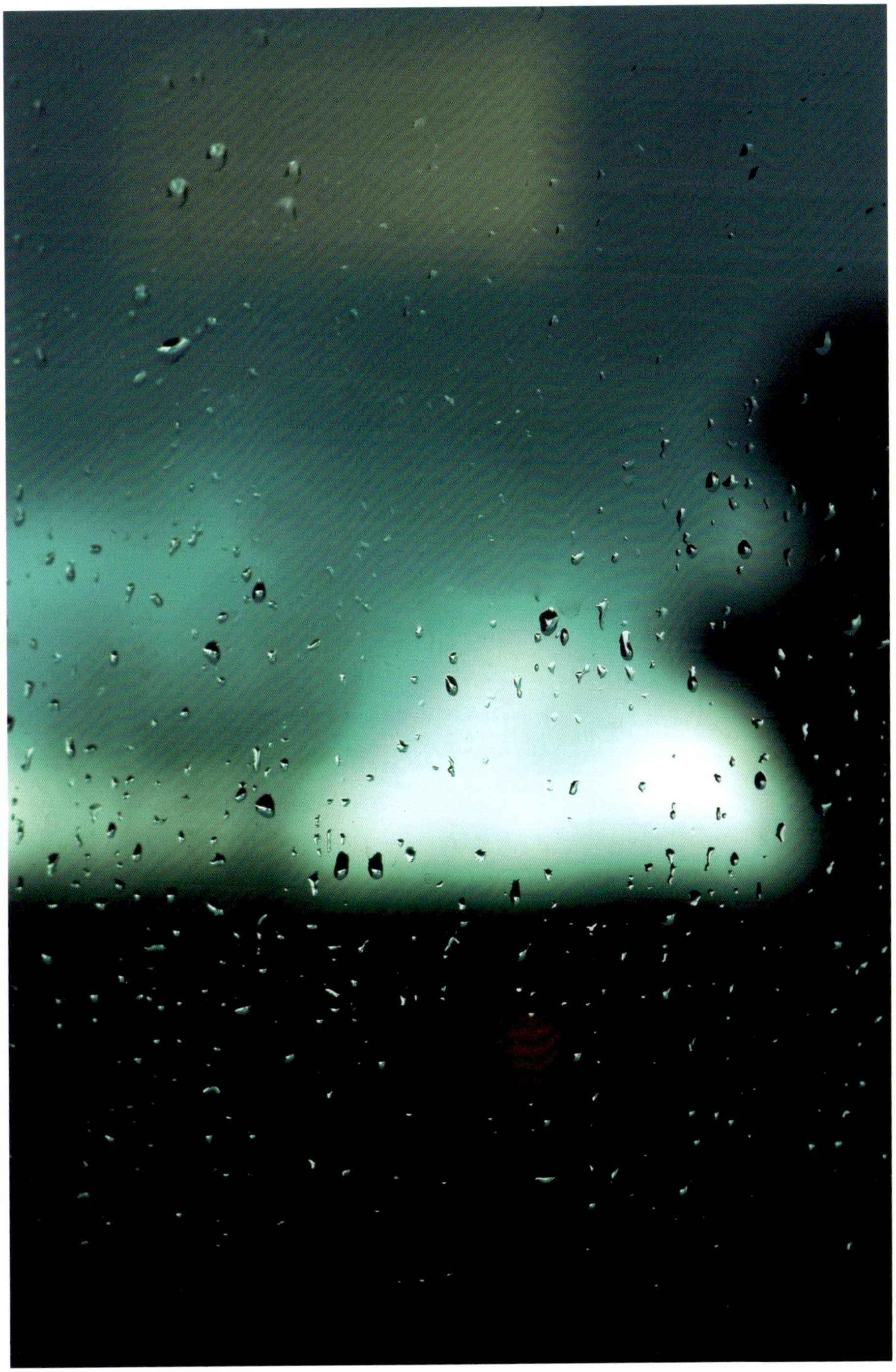

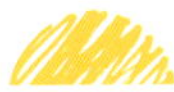

Siódma rano w tramwaju do Tallaght

Przełożyli Justyna i Cathal McCabe

Nie wiedziałem, że Zachód wyglądać będzie tak:
Znowu zasypiam w tramwaju o świcie.
Z moich ust już zniknął pocałunku twego smak.

Tak wiele tu języków, „zmęczenia" w nich nie brak.
W oknie senne twarze wpatrzone w nowe życie.
Kto wiedział, że Zachód wyglądać będzie tak?

Kto wiedział, ze będziemy zarabiać byle jak?
Codziennie o was myślę, o tym co robicie.
Z moich ust już zniknął pocałunku twego smak.

Przez telefon wyczułem w głosie twoim strach.
Czy na święta ty i dzieci do mnie przylecicie?
Nie wiedziałem, że Zachód wyglądać będzie tak.

Czy dla was się zmieniłem w comiesięczny czek?
Tyle buduję domów, żadnego nie kupicie.
Z moich ust już zniknął pocałunku twego smak.

Przerzucając cement, w moich skrytych snach
Całuję twoje ciało, jedyne na świecie.
Nie wiedziałem, że Zachód wyglądać będzie tak.
Z moich ust już zniknął pocałunku twego smak.

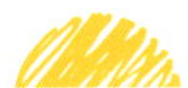

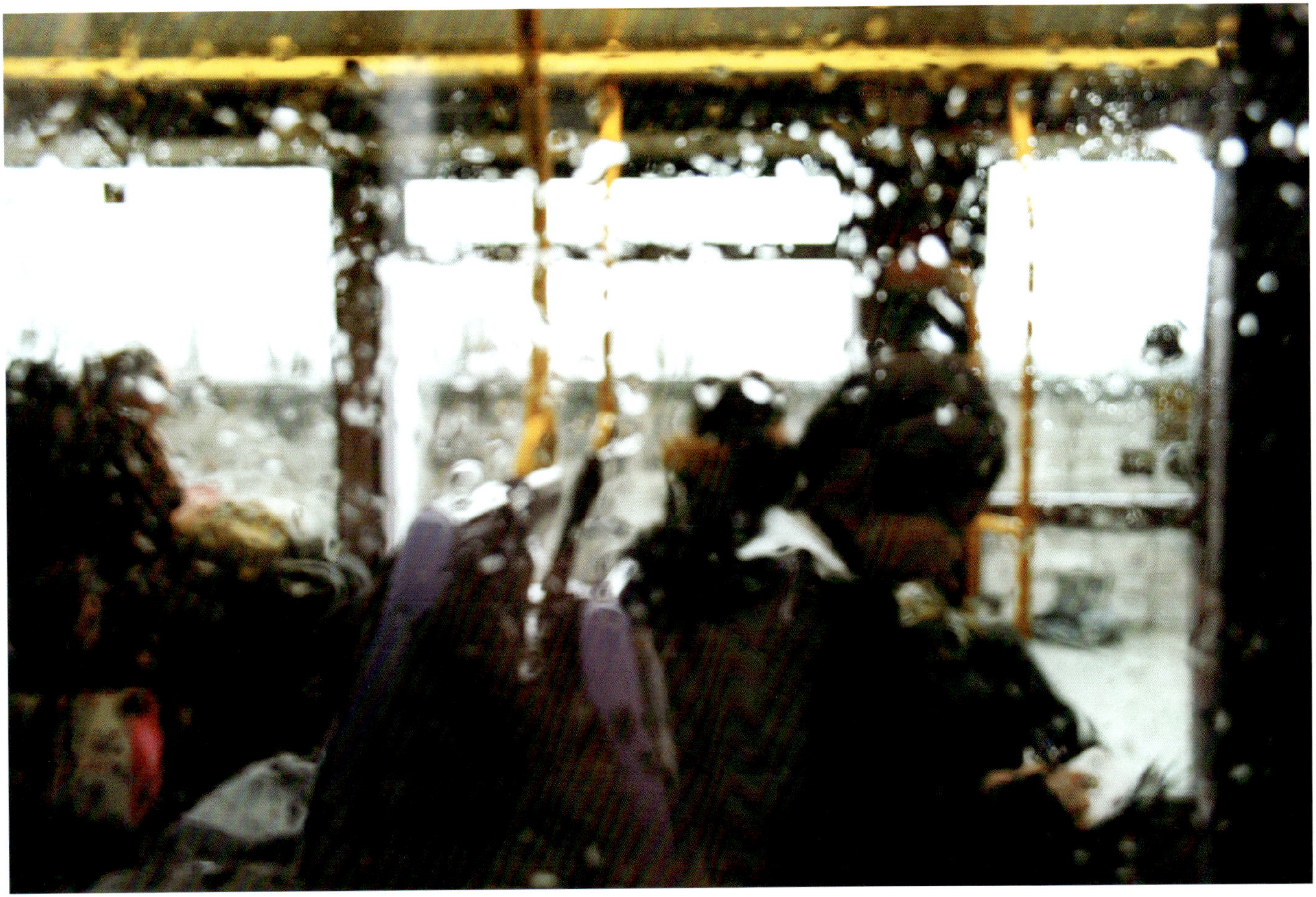

Warriors

Eileen Casey

The Grand Canal is silvery as a new coin.
I'm on the Luas thinking of nothing in particular
when a man, swift as an antelope,
runs from the houses towards Suir Road.

Legs, long as spears, gather speed
this Luas is a wild one

broken free from the herd.

On the grass, thawing frost steams a mirage,
dust rises.
His winter coat, shirt and navy trousers
dissolve to gorgeous Maasai colours.
He gleams like the skin on these tracks,
each muscle and sinew
zig zagging a perfect quarter arc

bearing down on the metal beast
and I'm back on the Midland streets

side-stepping pools of greenish-
hued cow dung. Straw
straggles from trailers, haggling
wasps swarm around my ears.

A cow breaks from a loose bunch,
is chased by a farmer in breeches
held up with braces, his face berry red,
legs akimbo; the stick in his hand
orchestrating a fair day.
Later, there'll be whiskey in the pubs
chocolate for children of the tribe
creeping in to sit on the long benches.

My warrior comes on board
scarcely out of breath. Beyond
Rialto
Fatima
St. James
Heuston Station

we journey towards the city.

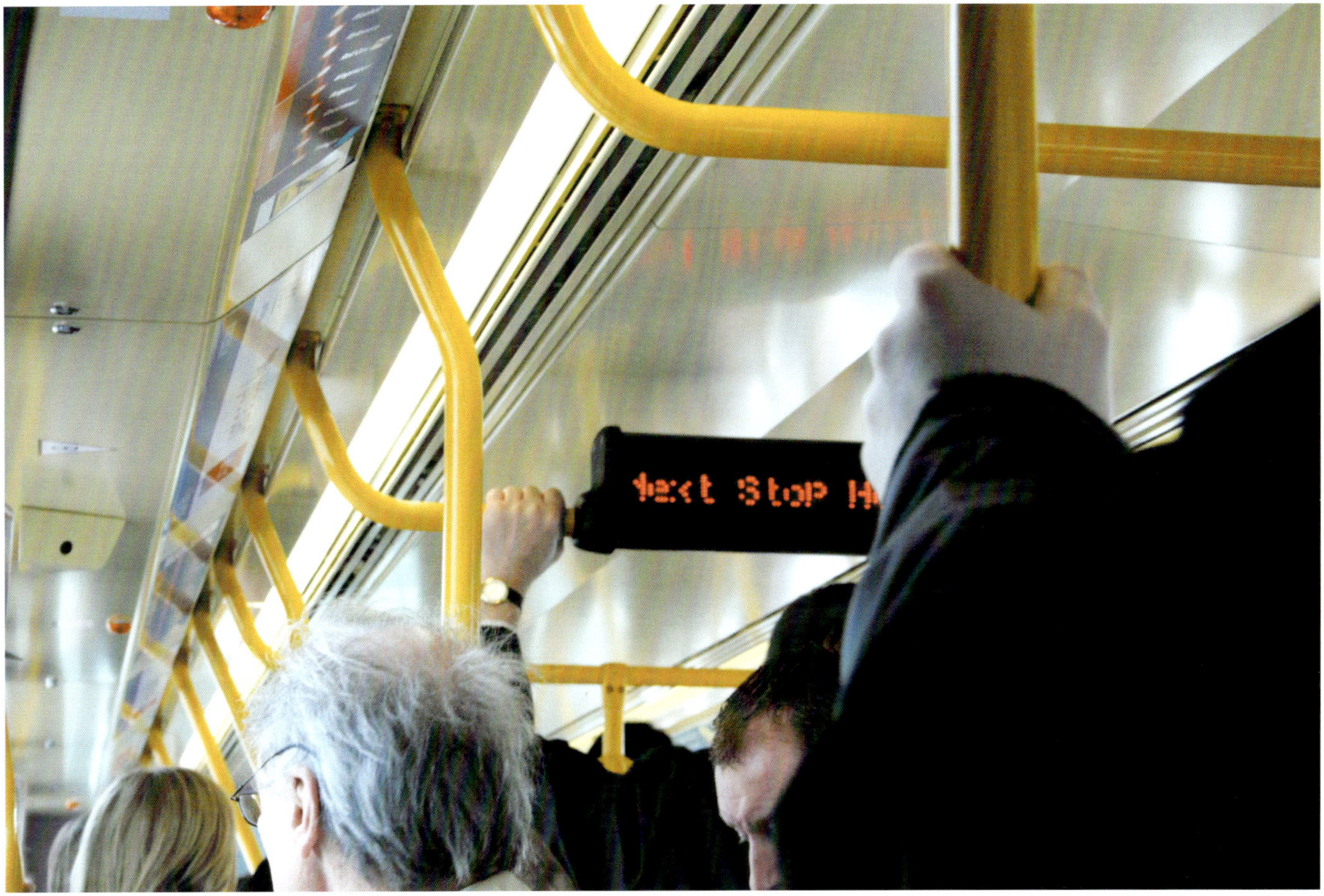

Woman Waiting for the Luas, Tallaght, 8.20am

Dermot Bolger

Collect my black skirt from the dry cleaners,
Then party napkins, potty trainers, crackers
For cheese and wine when parents collect
All of Sarah's new friends from the crèche:
Toilet rolls, paper towel to mop up party spills,
Foil-wrapped choc lollipops for going home bags,
Hoover bags, choc drops so our dog with bad breath
Won't start sighing, also feeling left out and slighted:
Sunday's dinner, a DVD I might persuade John to watch
When we're finally alone – his birthday princess put to bed:
Something, anything, to remind him then that I still exist.

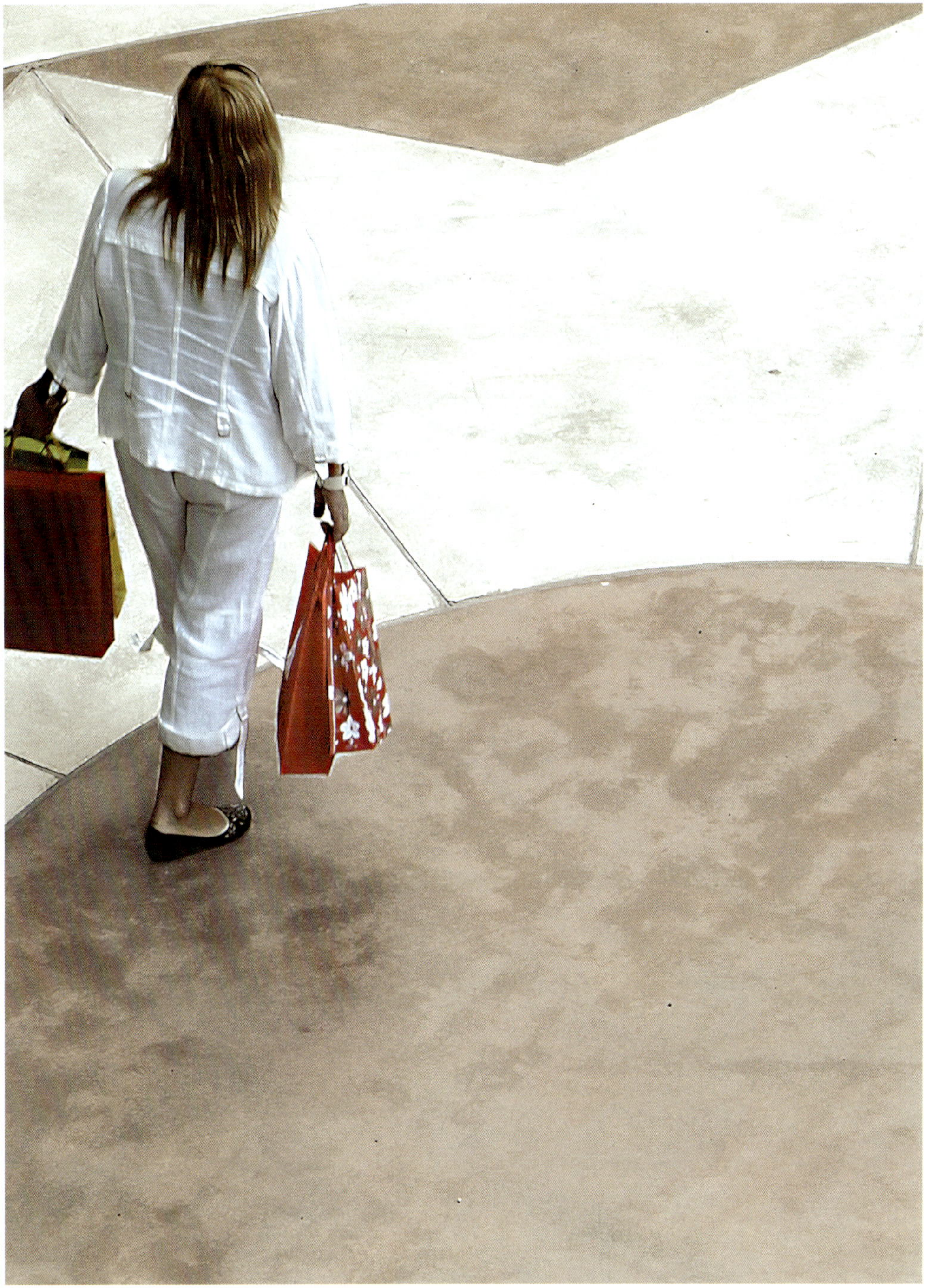

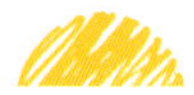

Bus Stop

Monica Carpenter

Shivering, I pace
While you stand,
Self-satisfied smile
On magenta lips
That match your coat,
Your delicate hands
Support collar beneath
Salon-expensive hair
Impervious to the
North-east winds.

Grounded, smug, aloof
You cast your gaze on me,
Assessing, automatically
I bow my head,
Out of sorts,
Out of time,
Out of place.

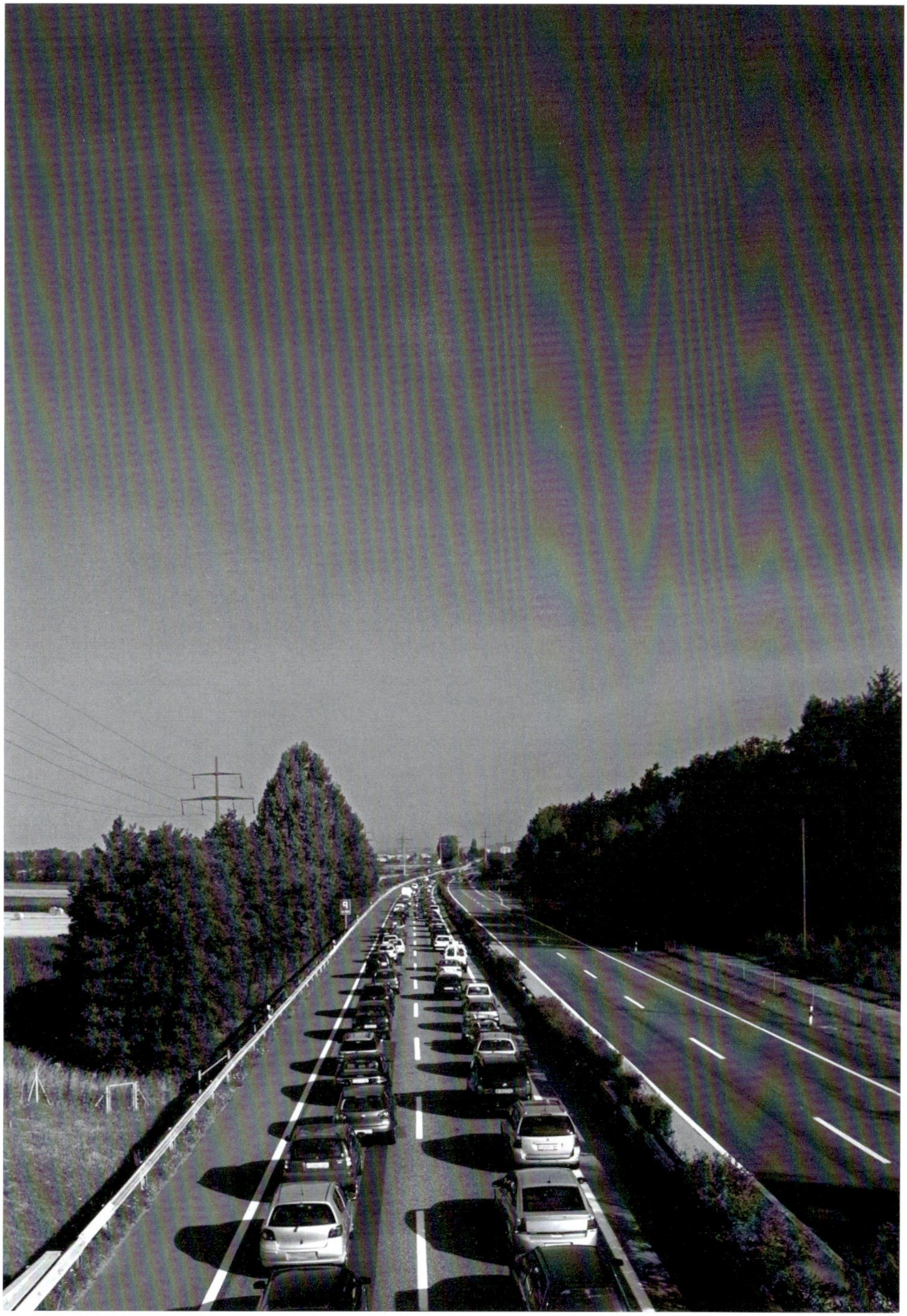

Living

Niamh Bagnell

9.30 pm – four soft soles, sole to sole we lie,
I'm sleepy, you're asleep.
Our toes keep in touch as we swim towards dreams,
Twitching, yelping, with eventual snores.
I giggle recalling the prelude
– my sexy striptease received by your reach
Not for condoms but for earplugs,
Sleep is the new sex.
We're paid 9 - 5, away from home 6 – 7.
Sleep is the new heaven.

We will get up in the morning –
Peel ourselves from the mattress.
Three snoozes after the first bell.
I listen to Chinese and Dan Brown as I drive,
Have given up reading in traffic jams,
Finally agreeing it's too dangerous.

You read about structures and language history
On your packed commuter bus.
Side by side with unknown neighbours.
Living on the edge
Of the city.

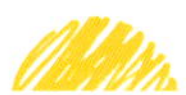

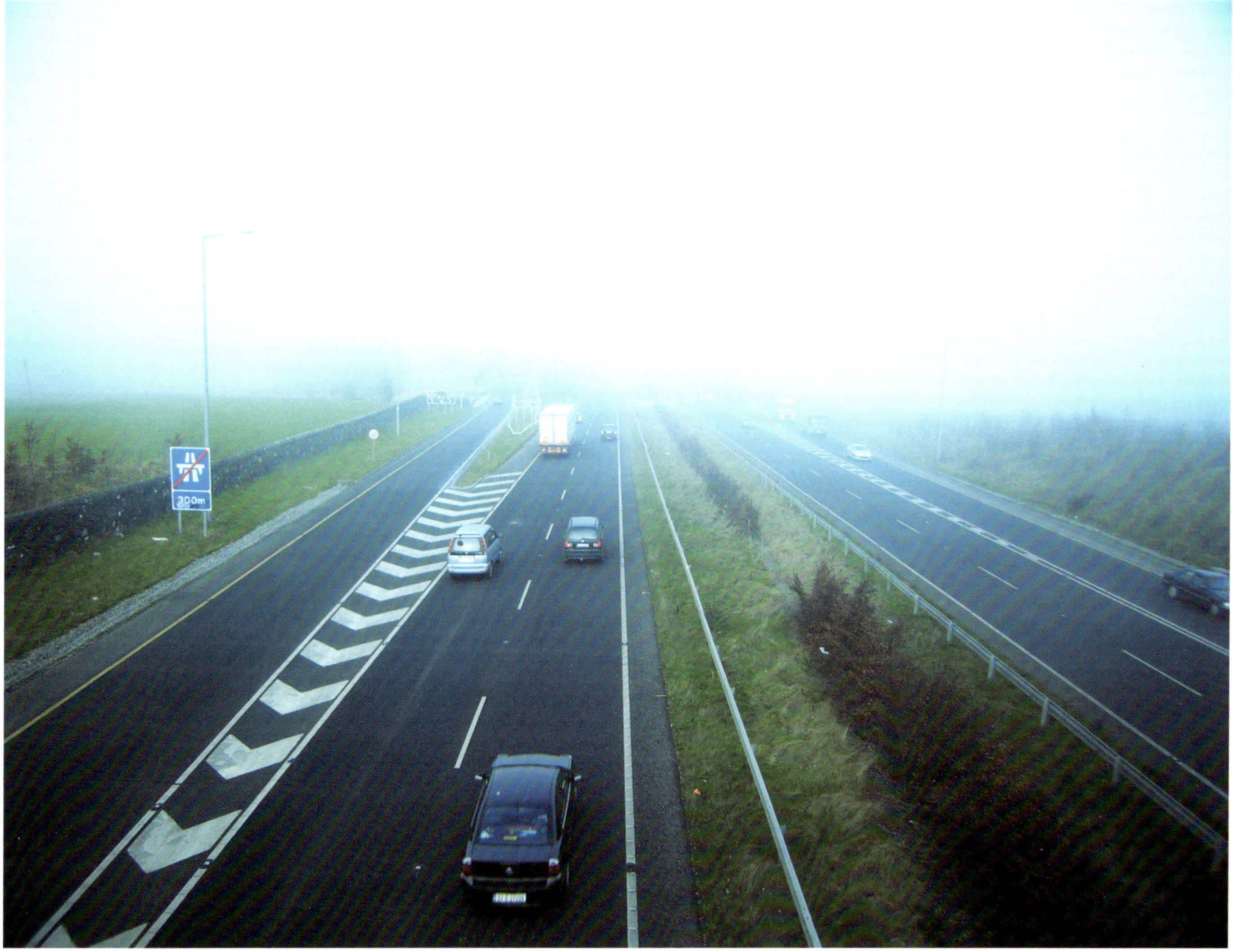

The Most Washed SUV on the Templeogue Road

Dermot Bolger

This is paradise, the only time that I truly own:
This solitary hour when I let my mind drift,

Stuck in this traffic, safe from her *"must do"* list
Pinned up in the kitchen with a fridge magnet.

Nobody notices me here as I hum favourite hits,
Fantasise about female motorists and recollect

The elation of struggling with straps, when girls
Let me undress them, frill by silky frill, on nights

When I was more constant than any Northern star,
When evenings brimmed with the possibilities

Of what fate might hold, what doors might open in bedsits,
Where kisses tasted of lipstick and Benson and Hedges.

Could I have envisaged then being captive in a car at dawn,
Content inside my prison, happy to be bullied and bossed,

Knowing that without my jailer I would be truly lost?
She controls time and motion until I strap on my seat belt

At eight a.m. – or earlier if I can invent reports of gridlock
When I arrive home at six she'll badger me out to the shed

That needs sorting, the lawn needing trimming, on her list
Where life can be ticked off into an ordered happiness.

Sometimes when she bends at the sink I want to lift her dress
Like that afternoon in her father's shed in her tennis skirt,

Only now she would tut and give me her *"act your age"* eyes.
I don't want to be my age, I want to sit here and fantasise

About convent girls or curing cancer or scoring tries
With a packed crowd hysterical in the corner where I lie

Bruised and sore, but ready to hold the ball aloft
Amid jubilant team mates, with the Triple Crown won,

Cures found for blindness, malaria, middle-age disgruntlement,
The mystery unsolved of the burglar who stole her fridge magnet,

Struggles with bra clasps at seventeen, fishnet stocking worn
By a Leitrim girl in a Rathgar flat, the illicit taste of woodbines,

A hand under the table in Zavargo's Nite Club, mysterious rust
Affecting the tools in our shed, with even the lawn-mower bust,

Our garden gone to pot, a power-cut and her whisper: *"I'm scared,*
Let's go to bed by candlelight. With no other heat in our residence

We must burn my to-do list to stay warm, unless you've other ways
To keep me warm, like on that afternoon I wore a tennis skirt,

And was correcting your pronunciation of 'Duice' when you grasped
Me tight about the waist in the shed amid Daddy's potting plants."

Her sweetness to which I surrounded everything, except my daily fix
Of sitting here staring at taillights, with no boss to supervise

This off-duty hour when I truly exist – midway between my desk
And henpecked life – the hero of the story, free to do as he likes.

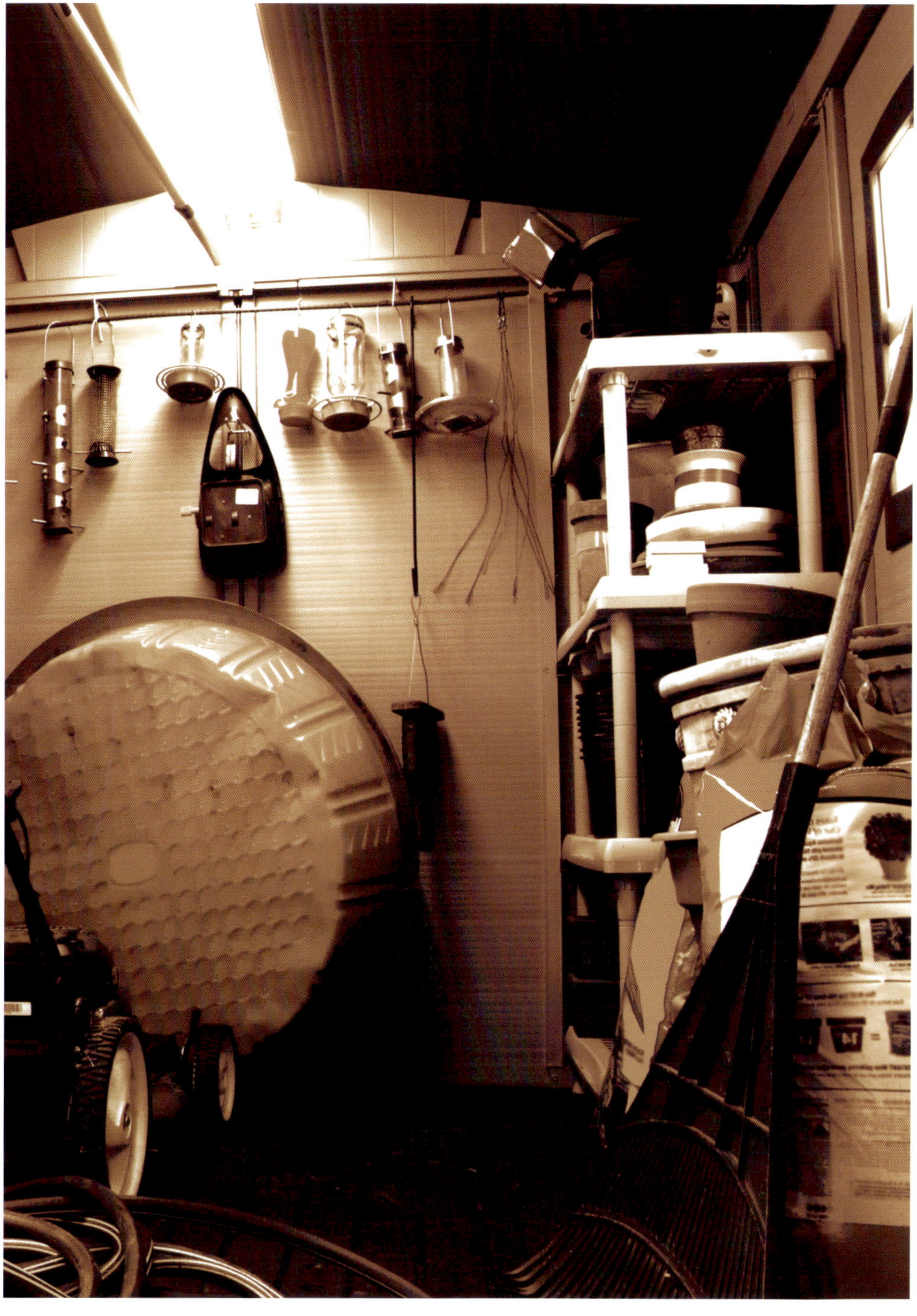

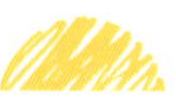

Yummy Mummy

Marie Gahan

I seem to spend my life behind this wheel
Mum's taxi's always at their beck and call.
My SUV is losing its appeal.

I don't get time to digest any meal;
School, swimming, ballet, judo and football,
I seem to spend my life behind this wheel.

Their rear-seat squabbles warrant nerves of steel
To stop myself from heading for a wall.
My SUV is losing its appeal.

The mileage I clock up is just unreal;
Bumper-to-bumper, like a snail we crawl.
I seem to spend my life behind this wheel.

My mirror shows the boredom they both feel
Each time I need to stop off at the mall.
My SUV is losing its appeal.

I'm late already for my Derma-Peel
And haven't made the gym this week at all.
I seem to spend my life behind this wheel,
My SUV is losing its appeal.

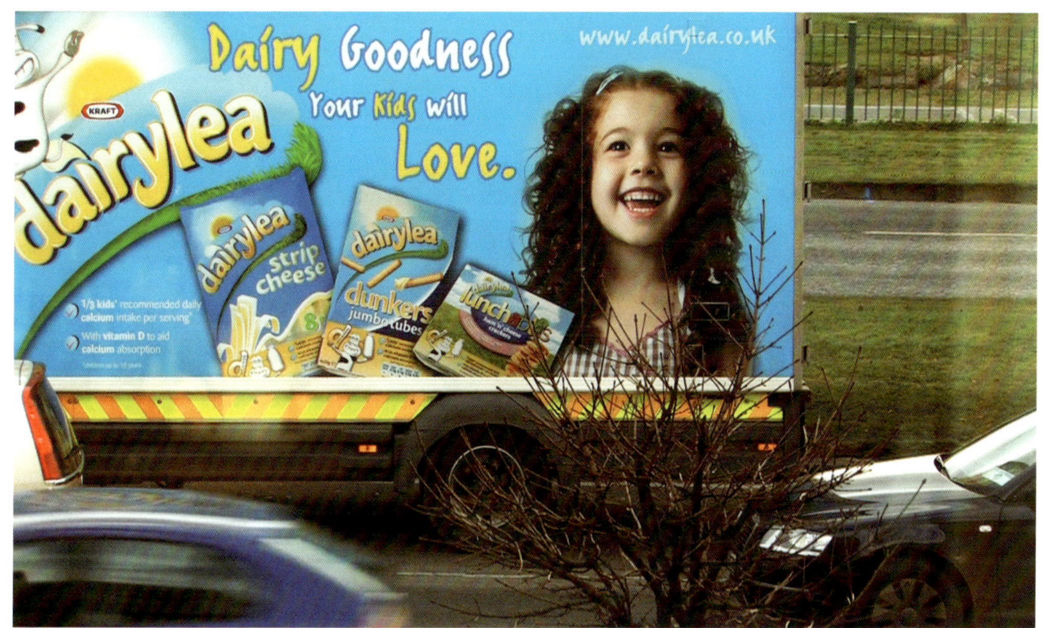

Dairy Goodness
Your Kids will
Love.
www.dairylea.co.uk
KRAFT
dairylea
1/3 kids' recommended daily calcium intake per serving*
With vitamin D to aid calcium absorption
dairylea
strip cheese
dairylea
dunkers
jumbo tubes

The Swimmer at Thirty-Five

(For Caroline Orr)

Dermot Bolger

The moment I hit the water I am in my element:
I was born for this, for backstroke and butterfly.
Born to hold my breath for the entire first length,

During which I slide out from my everyday skin
To again become a Leinster Schoolgirl champion,
All Ireland gold medallist and Olympic contender.

On childhood mornings in my father's old banger
There was no traffic like this, nobody else awake,
Just the pair of us wrapped up in a code of splits

In the pool that opened early just to let me train.
Chlorine and silence, the sense of being special,
The clarity of light when I stepped into the dawn

With the world only half-wake, as groggy-eyed
As the commuters now look in this tailback of traffic.
But while everyone looked stale, I never felt more alive

Then donning my school uniform to sit at a desk,
Reciting lap-times, my skin glowing with such health
That I could not envisage being daunted by any task.

I'd no time for boyfriends and barely time for friends.
Classmates marveled at how I coped with having no life,
But *that* was my life, I could imagine no existence then

Outside of that cocoon controlled by a stopwatch,
Where all problems were solved by simply going faster.
The lane kept clear, nothing allowed to block my path,

No tantrums, no silences, no waiting lists for doctors,
No grammar of autism to slowly learn to comprehend,
No son terrified of swimming, even with armbands,

Cocooned in his world that contains no stop-watches,
No sense of time, no admittance granted to strangers.
I drive my child to day-care centres and specialists

On choked roads like this and while I curse the traffic
He stares out blankly as if half watching a dull film.
I love him and he loves me, even if he cannot show it.

In some dreams I see him dive into a pool and glide
In my slipstream, made graceful by a floating world.
But he screams if he even sees me pack my swim gear.

In my local pool strangers stare twice a week, transfixed
By my apparent speed. But to me it feels like slow motion
As I blunder into beginners who block up my lane.

Why bother wasting my precious hours of parole there?
Perhaps because, occasionally amid a tumble-turn
I block out this constant sense of impeded helplessness,

And become the perfect swimmer, effortlessly omnipotent,
Moving with ease, barely needing to draw breath:
Where no disappointment can touch me in my element.

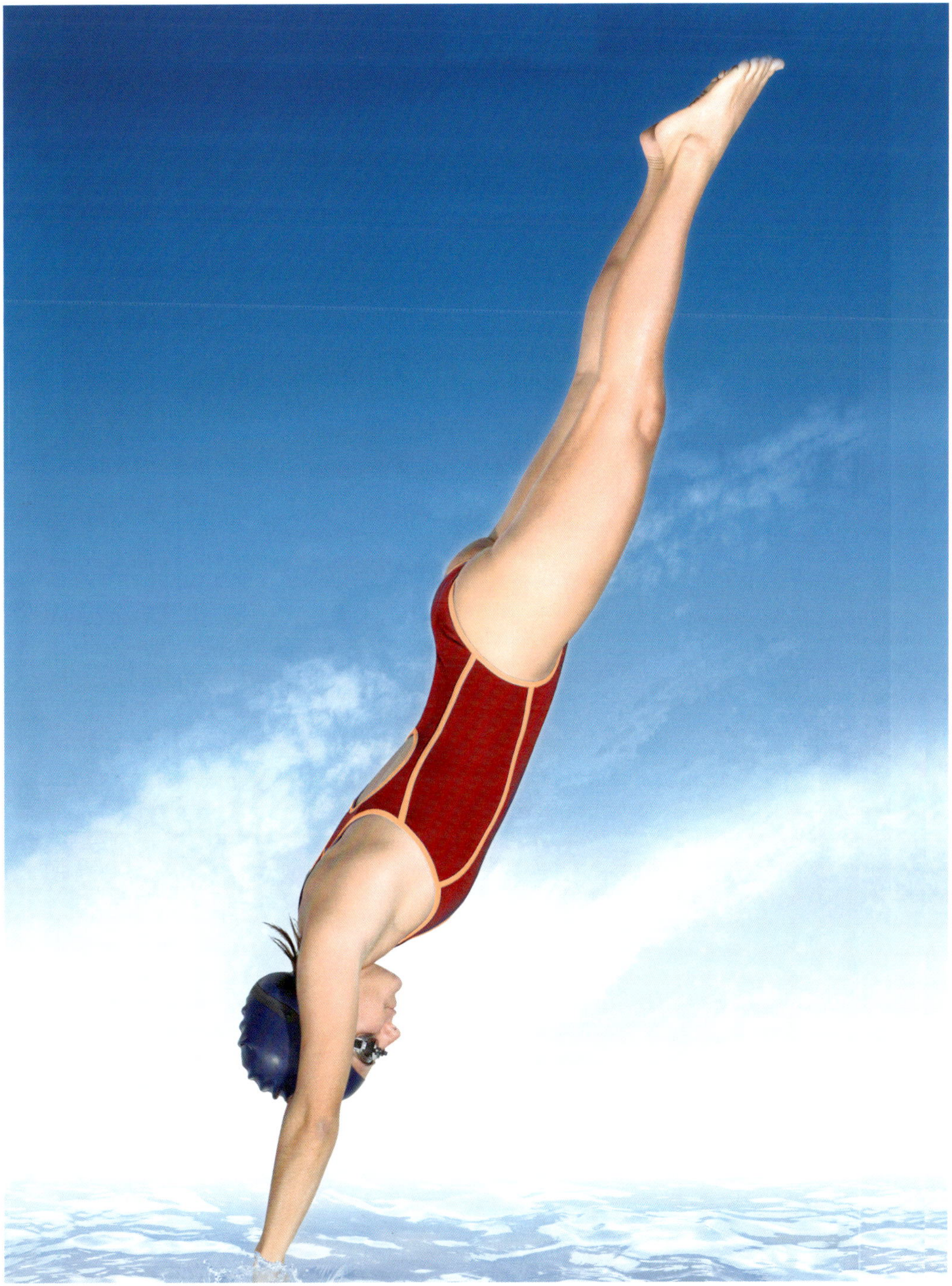

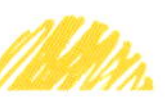

Question

Blathnaid Nolan

I have a daughter,
A beautiful daughter
With dark blue eyes
And chestnut hair.

I have a son,
A golden son
With long brown lashes
And a clear soft voice.

I have a daughter,
A simple child
Who has struggled
To walk, talk and play.

I have a son,
A clever boy
Who sails through life
With blessed ease.

I have a child
Who loves everyone
And for whom the phone
Never rings

I have another,
A popular boy,
Invited to all
The birthday parties.

I have friends,
Upstanding people
Whose children prefer
Another playmate.

I have a son
Who accepts without question
Simple minds
And twisted limbs.

I have a pain
Born from knocking
On the closed doors
Of busy friends.

I have a question,
Would I have been
So very different?

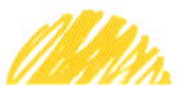

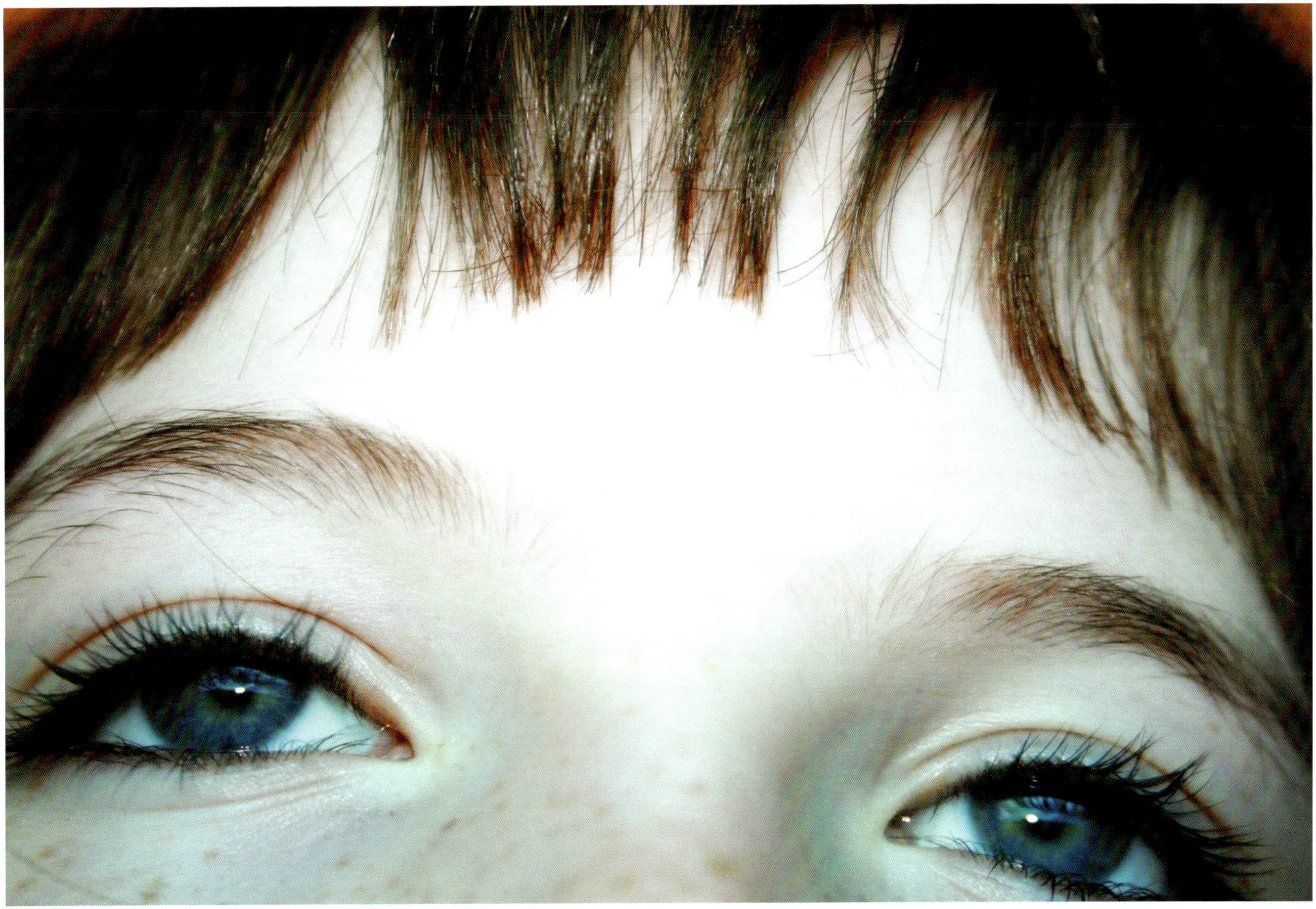

Lucan Weir

Dermot Bolger

Will you walk with me here, beside Lucan weir,
Past flowering rush, kingfishers, green figwort,

Your palm so young in mine, your palm frayed with age:
Each generation a whirling leaf sluiced into this cascade.

Will you recall the ordinary afternoon when we paused,
Amid the rush of busy lives, to stare at the torrential spume,

Hypnotised by the ceaseless deluge, until in fact it seemed
That what remained constant and static was this surging weir,

With all our joys, our dreams, our lives spiralling past,
Down each speeded-up season, each irreclaimable year.

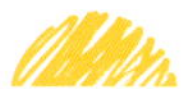

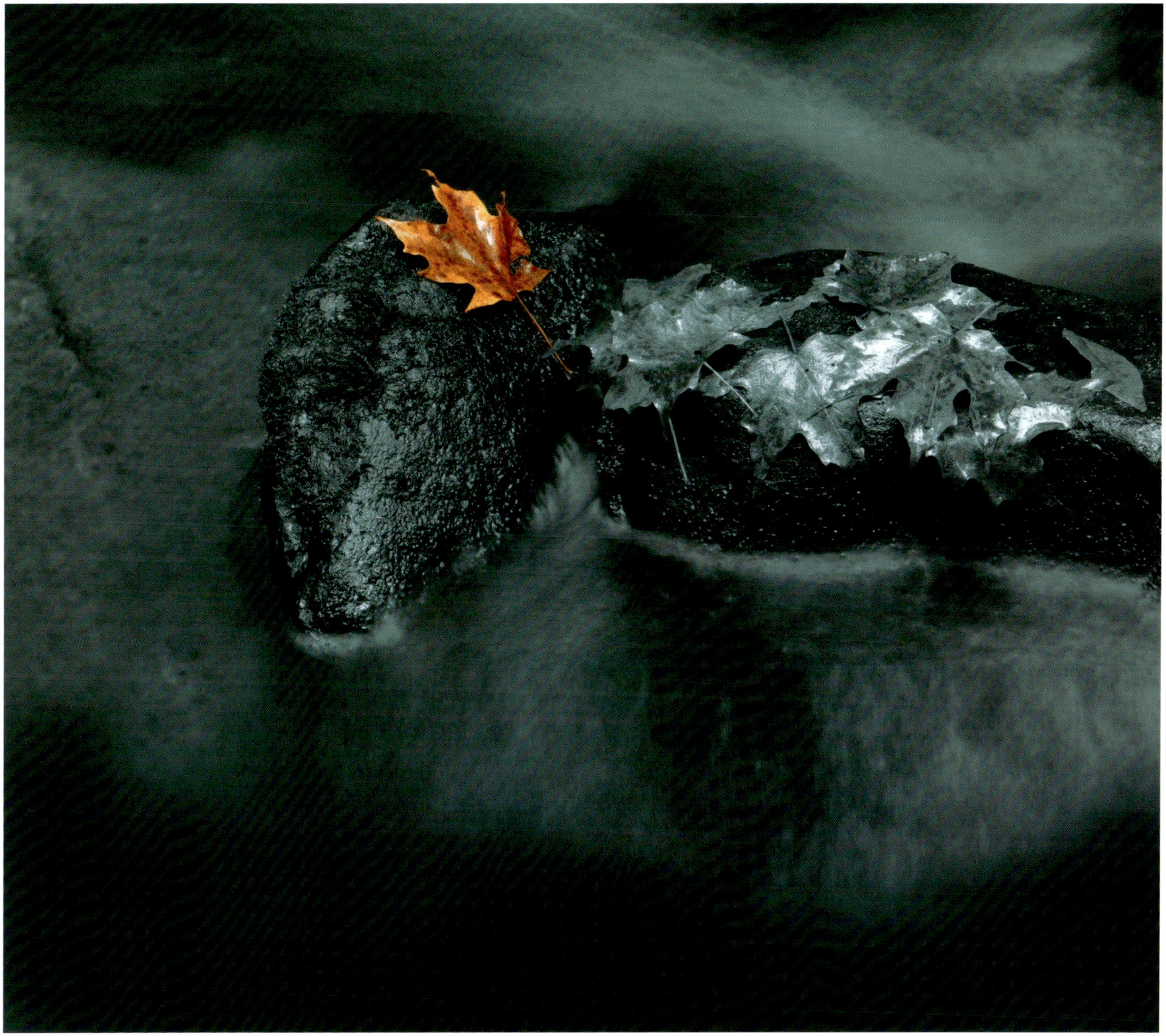

To School and Back

(for Martha)

Brian Kirk

Your second year already
And my first as your daily guide.
Your little hand in mine,
We walk the quarter mile in silence,
Just two amid a stream of others,
Part of the crowd, but separate.

In the yard the children
Form straight lines and wait
In expectation of the class;
The first constraint – the first sign
Of the hand of man upon the face of God
After the fall in Eden.

I watch your peerless image fade,
Eclipsed by Plato's puppet forms.
A door closes (perhaps another opens
Somewhere in return), and you are gone.
The morning's mine to think of you
And wait till half past one.

I hear the angels' voices rise and fall,
Benediction through an open window.
And then a sudden tumult, an energy released,
The angels beat their wings upon the glass
Until the gates of heaven open and she is there
Before me, smiling, telling me her life.

Your little hand in mine,
We walk the quarter mile in silence,
Just two amid a stream of others,
Part of the crowd, but separate.
You run ahead when we attain our street,
The fallen leaves are gold stars at your feet.

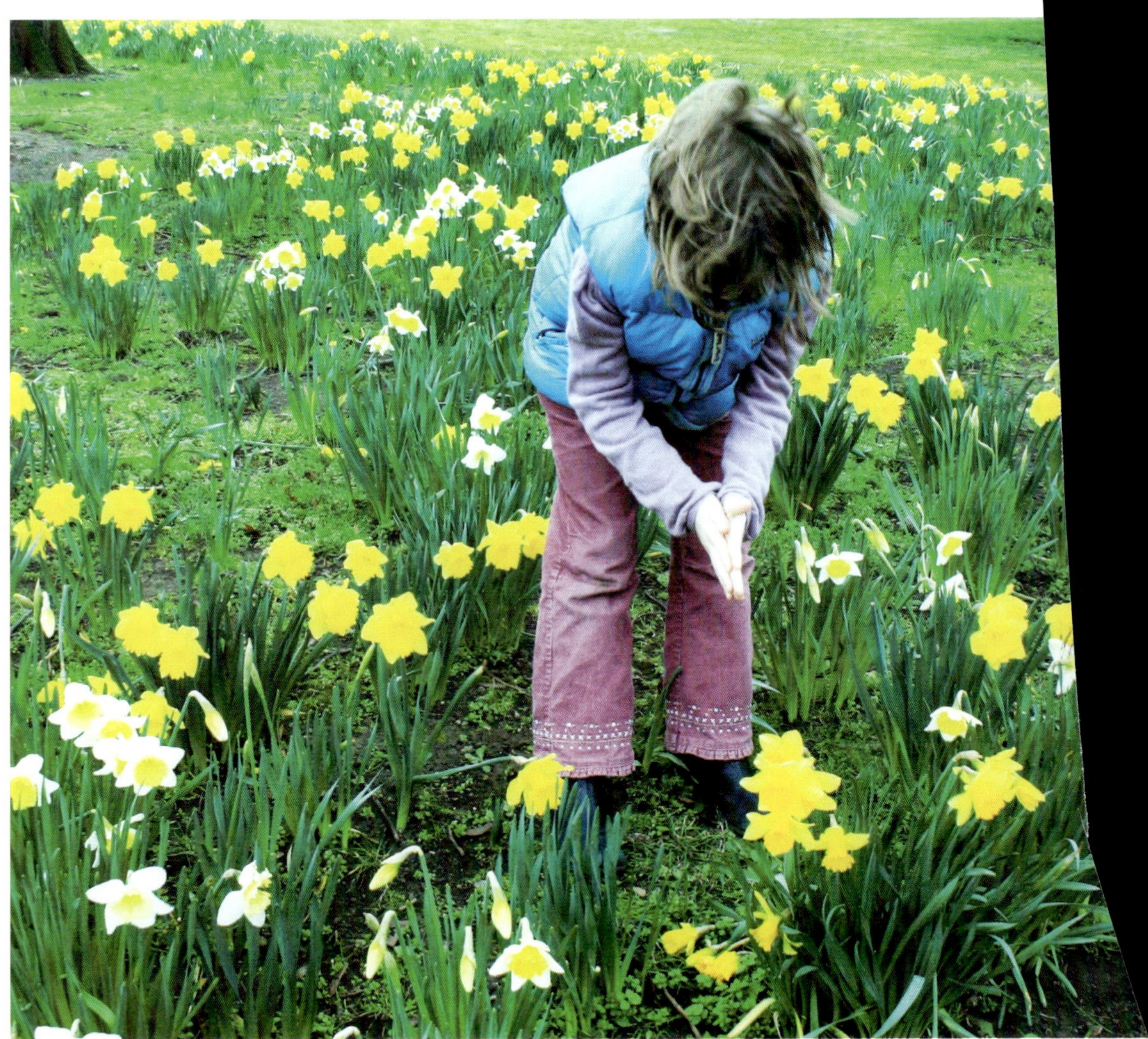

Grange Castle Haiku

Kate Dempsey

My headlamps light up
The burnt down Pollyhops pub
Now fired by sunrise

End of summer term
No multi-ethnic bus queues
In blue uniforms

Reports on the news -
Shattered glass and broken lives
Tyre tracks on the verge

I am late for work -
I park amid the stragglers
Halfway to Tallaght

Low maintenance shrubs,
Designer style grass hillocks
Feed hares and rabbits

Men wait with airguns –
Some nights they send in the dogs
Flush game out the gates

Tabby cat's tail whips,
Baby rabbit in her jaws -
We pause, traumatised

Half a V - four swans
Fly straight over the power lines.
Where are they going?

Health and Safety bleat -
Walk don't run, hold the hand rail
Don't fall and sue us

Sunshine at lunchtime
We slip from shadowed buildings
Winter pale faces

Phelim wants Mark's job,
Mark's more than a match for Niamh
Niamh's soft on Phelim

Maria comes in –
We stop googling cheap breaks
Change screens to spreadsheets

Here are no seasons –
We wear the same clothes year round,
Watch weather through glass

Cathal winks at me
Chats up the girls in QA
We'll do all he asks

What a wasted day -
The afternoon spent fixing
The broken morning

Evening's clock hand crawls
Minute to dawdled minute
Time treacles to five

The sun shines all day -
Clouds roll in from Dublin Hills
By five it's raining

Luke waits in the rain
Dreaming of his driving test
Until the bus comes

My contract's up soon -
This plant will still be working -
I'll be somewhere else

Hi-tech glass building
I pinch myself as I leave -
This is where I work.

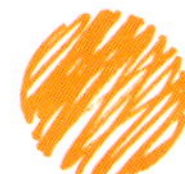

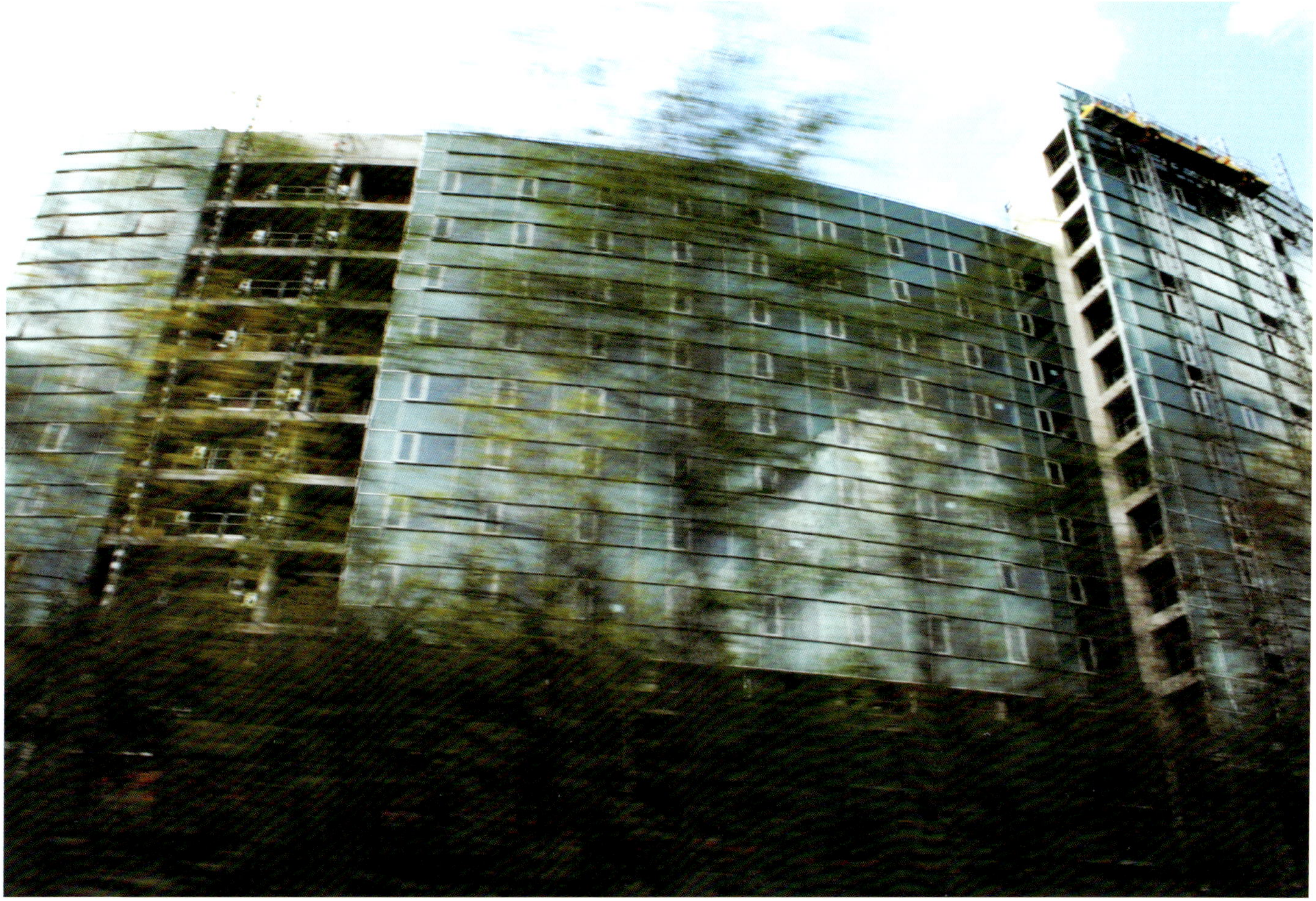

In a Clondalkin Supermarket Car Park

Dermot Bolger

Screw all self-appointed martyrs,
Ignore their beguiling monuments:
Screw any ghosts with the neck
To impose upon their descendants
The mortgage of any emotive debt,
Any cloying duty of remembrance
That turns the past into an excuse
To hold us to ransom in the present.

Let the weight of history seem as light
As a party balloon slipping from the grasp
Of a child distracted in a crowded car park.
Let it float above cars choking exit lanes
Until tribal braves become blue specks,
So indistinct amid a skyline of cranes
That they cannot be hijacked from the grave
As tools to be used to justify or condemn.

The child watches her balloon disappear,
She does not stamp her feet or simper;
She lets the past go, being too enthralled
By all the possible futures that await her.

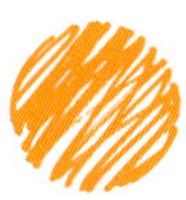

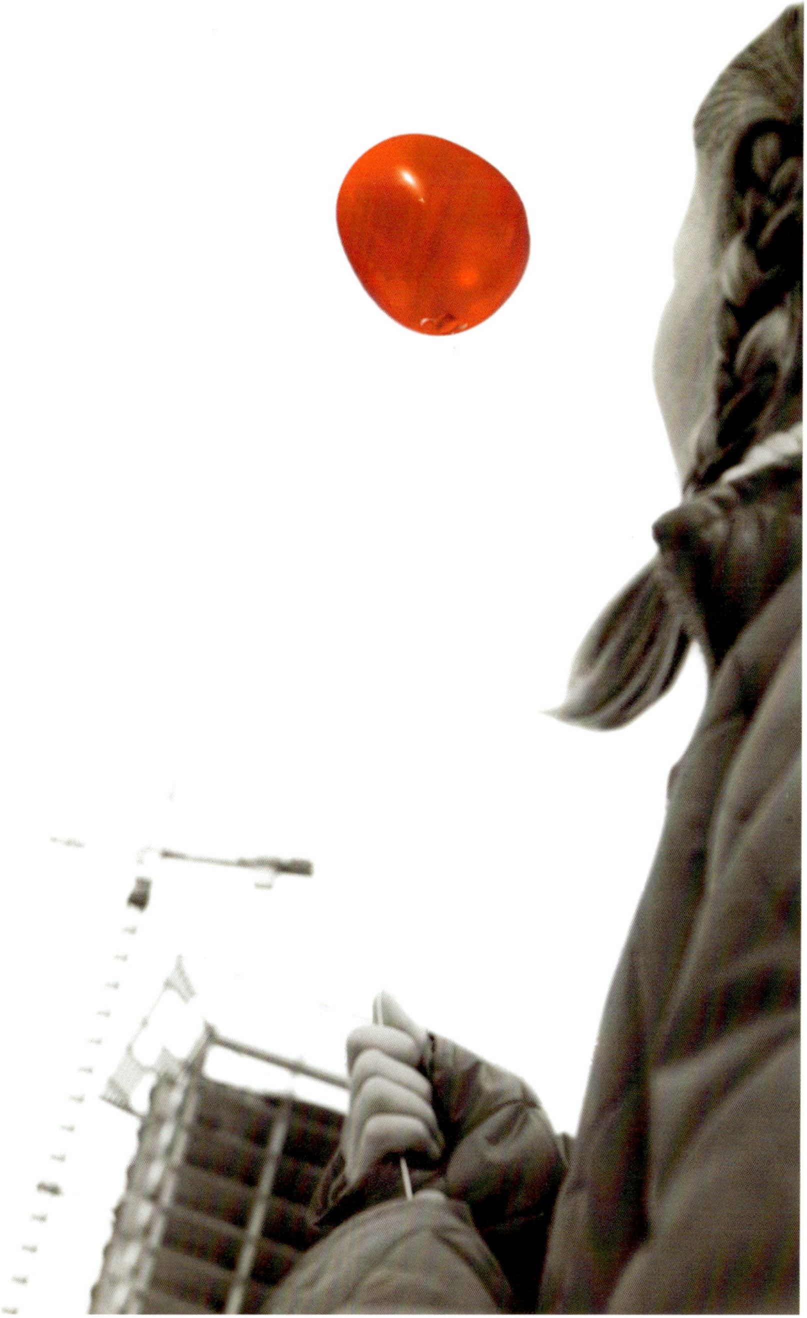

Nigerian Lady on Tallaght High Street

Siobhan Daffy

She wears indigo,
Oniko blue.

Adire headscarf
Tells a tale of old,

Squares of chequered gold
In a raffia stitch.

Silver circles in her ears
Spill tinkles of time.

Sun dark skin,
On her smiling cheek bones.

Her feet hug the ground,
Her hips at one

With the ebb and flow
Of the moon and the sun.

One child at her breast,
Another by the hand

Queen of this land.

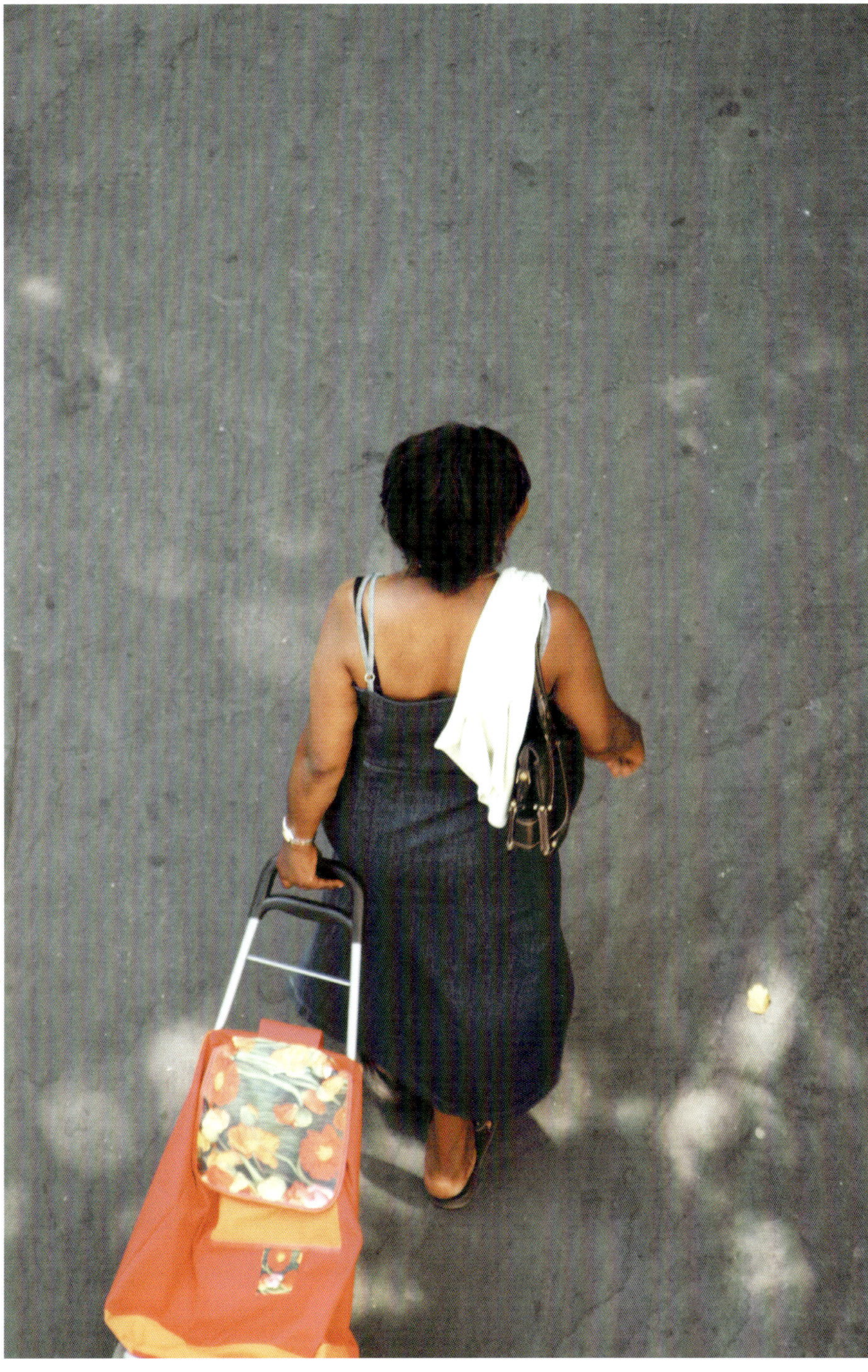

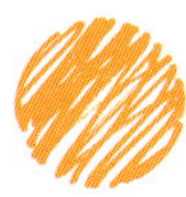

I am a Nigerian from West Africa

Adenice Adedoyin

When I first came to Tallaght it was difficult.
The buses were not regular.

Tallaght has been good - I can work
And call myself part of the community,

And Tallaght has been bad -
There were attacks from adults and teenagers.

Tallaght has been good and bad.

Today I call myself part of the community.
Today is a different story, I can work.

My job helps me know more about Irish people,
Their needs and feelings and beliefs.

I am a Nigerian from West Africa.
When I first came to Tallaght it was difficult.

The buses were not regular.
But every town has its ups and downs.

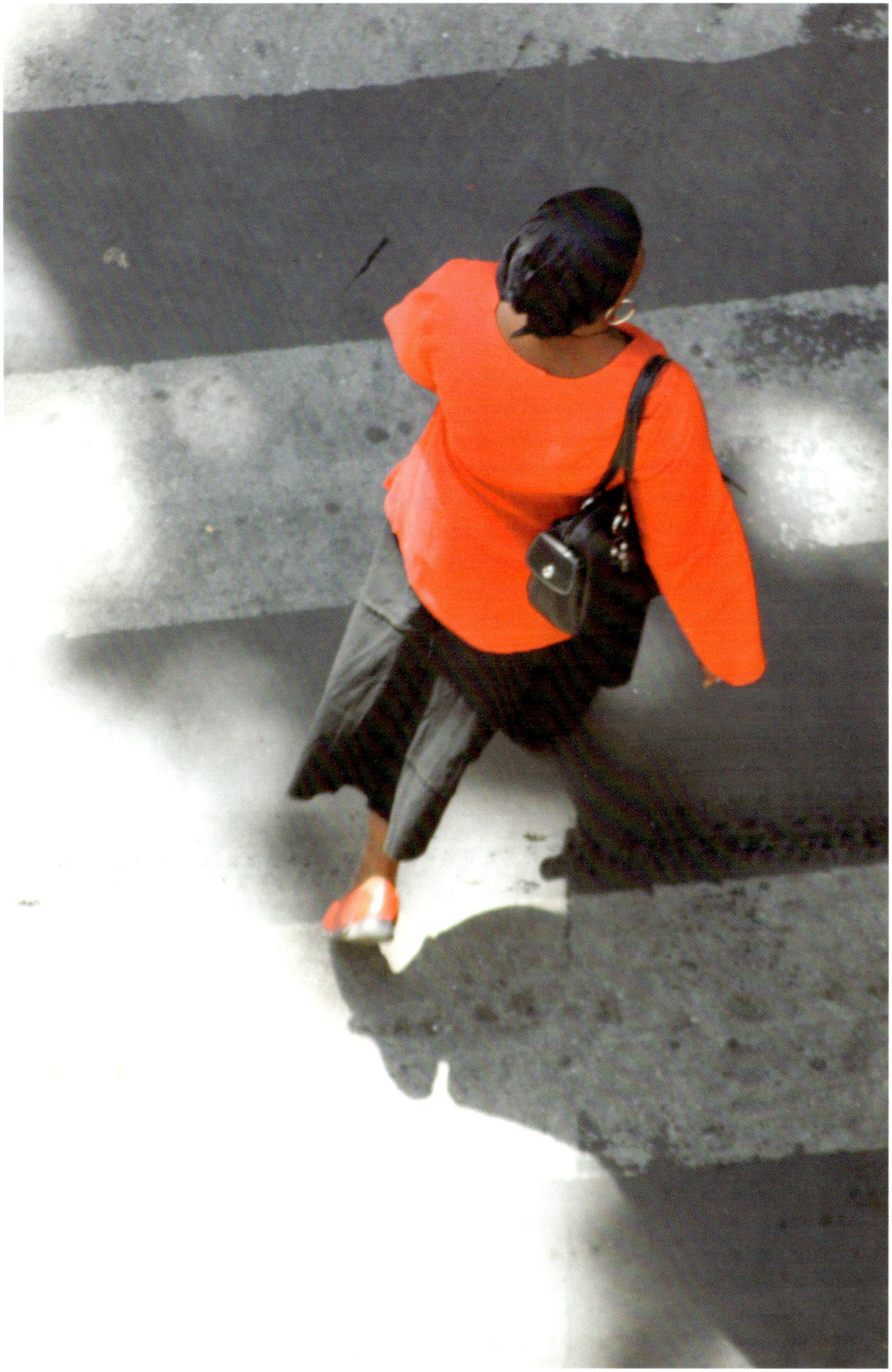

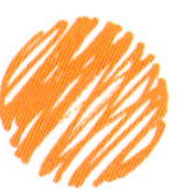

Neilstown Matadors

Dermot Bolger

Super models would kill to be this thin.
The diet is stress, cigarettes and coffee.
My child-raising days should be done,
But somebody had to step into the breach,
Somebody had to pick up the scarlet cloak
And hold it in front of the rampaging bull.

Old spectators in the bull rings of Mexico
Pay no heed to fearless young toreadors
Who imagine themselves to be invincible.
Their interest only stirs after a fighter is gored,
Because only when he re-enters the arena
Will they witness his true test of character.

Some afternoons after school in this room,
Waiting to see the Drugs Taskforce worker,
When my granddaughter suddenly smiles,
When she looks up from her colouring book
With eyes that match my daughter's eyes,
With eyes knowing nothing yet of the danger
Of dealers peddling needs that need to be fed,
With quizzical eyes that I would kill to protect,
She asks the question that she loves to ask:
"Gran, what did you do before you did this?"

What did I do before I took on her welfare?
I fought to raise a daughter on these streets,
I stood in queues and worked on checkouts,
I searched for my child on dangerous estates,
I stood up to debt collectors calling to my door,
When she shivered in detox I tried to nurse her,
I sold my possessions or saw them all robbed,
I cried until one night there were no tears left,
I prayed with what remained of my ebbing faith,
In time I wrapped my grandchild into my arms
And took the place of the person I loved most,
I made a nest amid the belongings I possess,
I stood up in the ring every time I was gored,
I watched the bulls run and raised my cloak
Repeatedly to provide what shelter I could,
I picked myself up and wiped off the blood,
I waited at the school gate to take her hand
So that, walking home, no evil could touch her.

I don't say such things as I stroke her fingers.
Instead I say, as her eyes widen with wonder:
"Every night during your ten years in this world
As you sleep I enter the bull ring with my sword
To stand where your mother would have stood:
A gladiator standing guard, a secret matador."

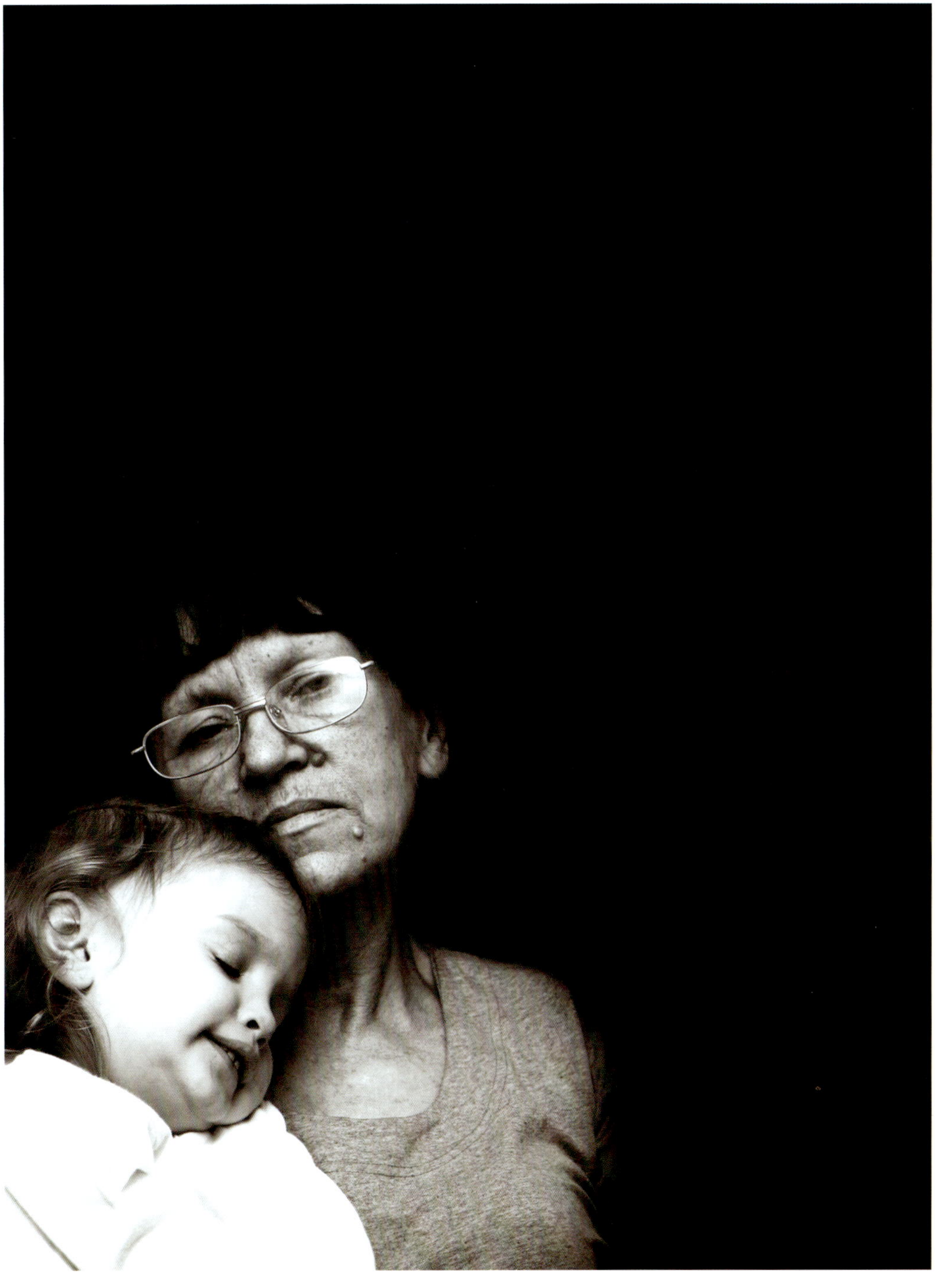

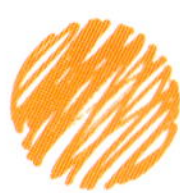

Quarryvale Community Centre

Eva Kelly

The Pied Piper camps in these walls.
Multi-coloured photographs,
Art projects, expressions of a rising generation,
Youth groups, Splash Art, Rainbow Club
And Q-Connection.

The teen counselling room is above this level,
Doors have fire proof glass.
Congested canteen every Wednesday
Especially between the hours of 3pm to 5pm
When the Drop In takes place.
The full Sports Hall
Quick to reprimand the slowest player.

In the active Art room
Stands a seven foot tall metallic robot
Made of recycled beer cans,
Smiling with plastic bottle tops for eyes,
The torso filled with tabloid newspapers
Wrapped tight,
Secured with chicken wire,
Like a high rank solider looking over
An assembly of Quarryvale's youth
Spanning from Shancastle to Greenfort
And reaching as far as Harelawn.

Outside these bright strong walls
A different kind of inferno blazes.
Skeletons gather at the local shops,
Another teenage suicide:

Death by misadventure.

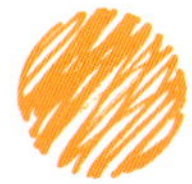

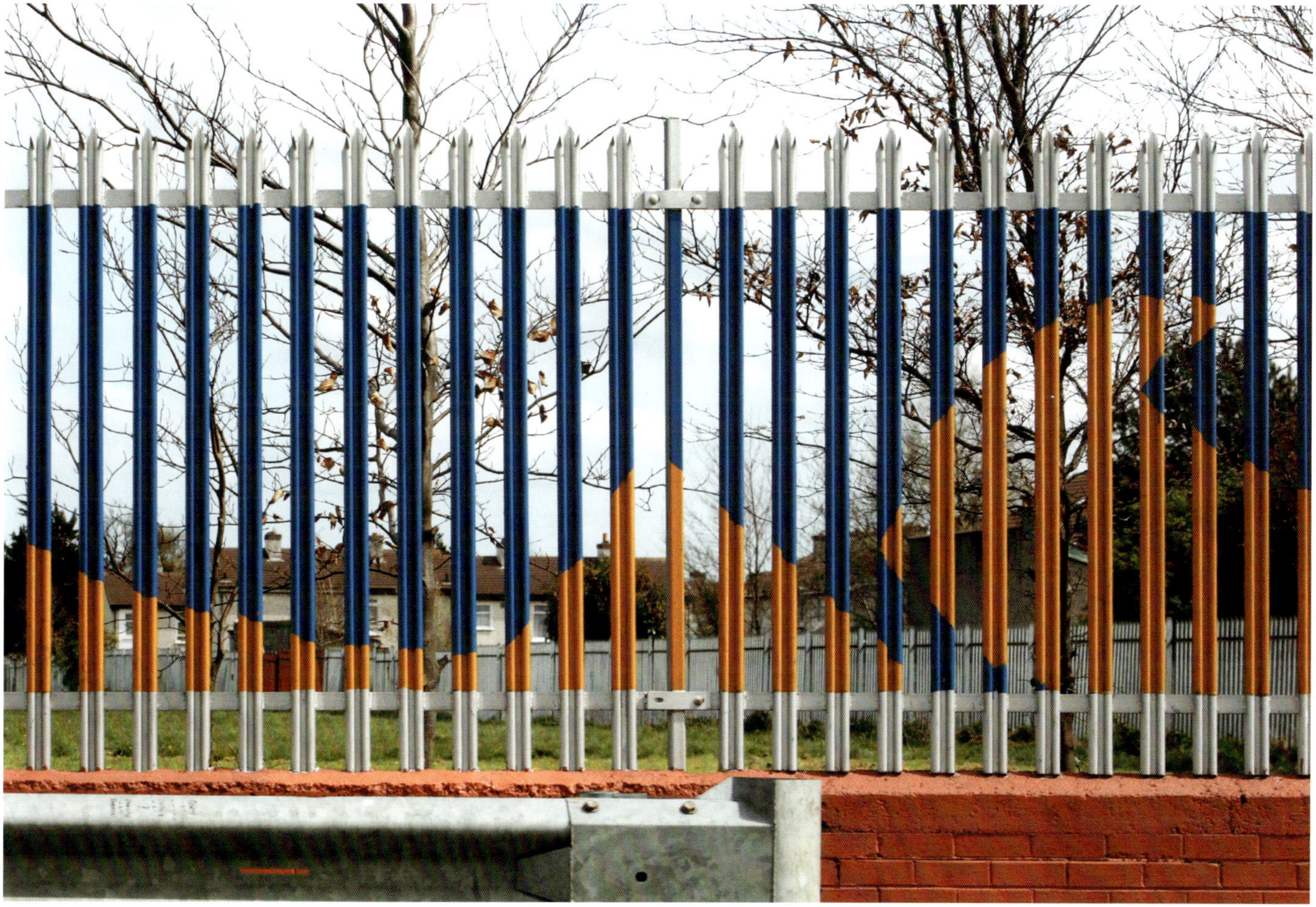

Girl, Fifteen, Walking in Ronanstown

Dermot Bolger

I am walking and I shall keep walking,
Past the gangs clustered on the corners
With nothing except catcalls and jeers,

Past shuttered shops where we kissed,
Past graffiti-strewn lanes we haunted
Before his betrayal soured their magic.

I am walking past interrogating stares,
An inquisition of girls with know-all eyes.

I am Nicky-No-Name, declining all labels,
Walking tall because I know my own worth.

I refuse to look down and refuse to look back,
I shiver from the cold but feel no regret,

Because I carry my destination in my heart,
Even if I lack the words to express it yet.

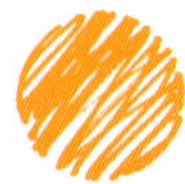

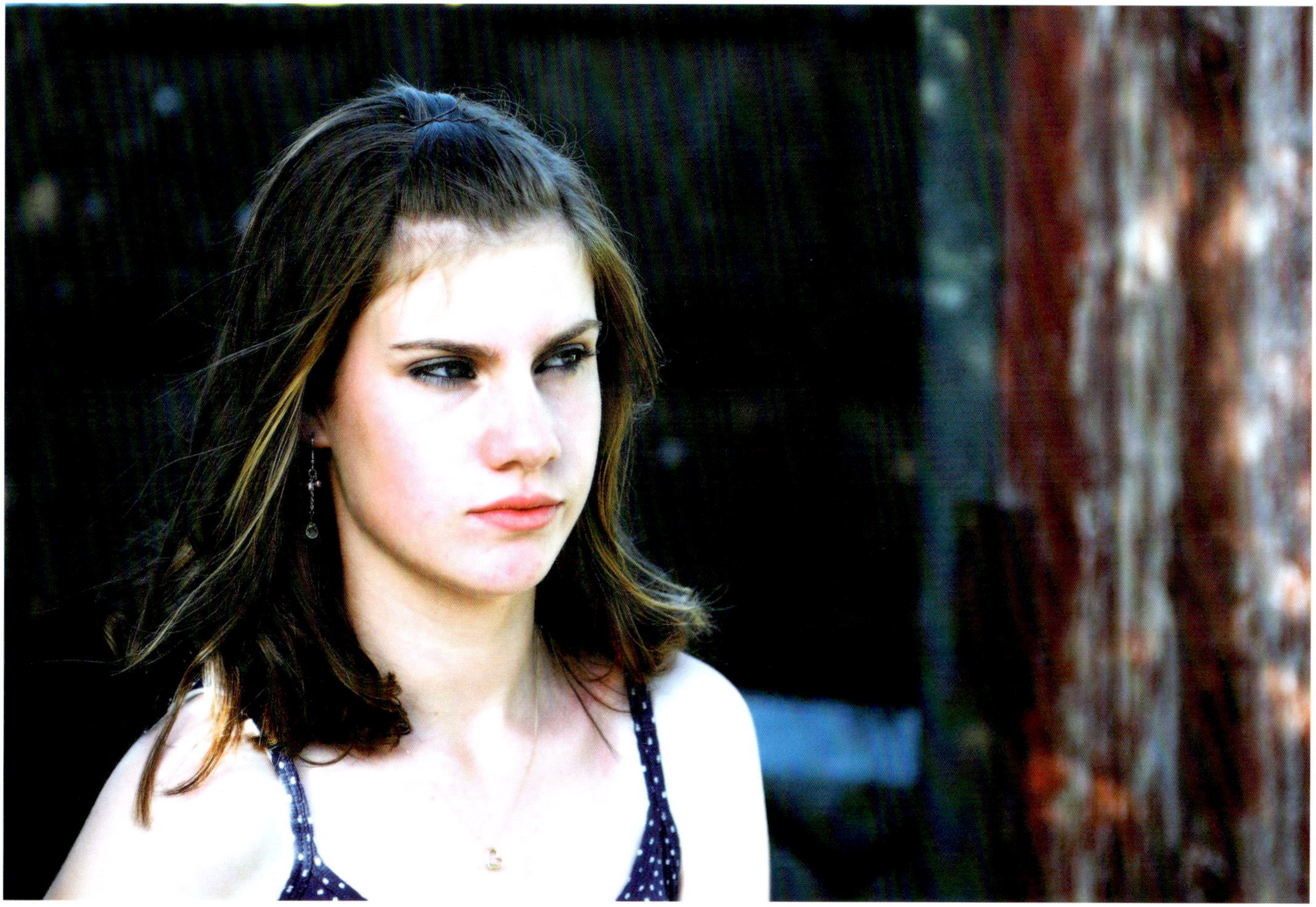

A Child in Fear

Bridget Connors

Fear in the life of a child
Will always stick in their memory.

For a long time now,
For as long as I can remember
I can remember such a fear.

Why would a woman who reared seven children,
Who had eleven – four who died at birth –
Why would she put up with such abuse?

Did she feel she was not good enough?
Did she feel she deserved no happiness?
These are the questions I ask all the time.

My Dad was a very bad man when he drank,
My Mum called him the Devil.
She would know when he was ready,

She would run and hide,
But he always found her
And boxed her and kicked her,

All because his horse came in last
And he had lost money.

She would hide her eye
Next day from the neighbours,
She always forgave him.

She hated when he got paid,
She knew he would drink
And she would get a hiding.

I remember the fear in her eyes,
She sometimes hid in the wardrobe
With her fingers in her ears.

Did a married woman in the 1960s
Think that was part of being a wife?
Getting kicked and hit?

My Mum's mother always said
If Mum went to her with a black eye,
"You made your bed, so lie on it."

What words to say to your child:
If my daughter's partner laid a hand on her
I would scald him with boiling water.

But how, I ask myself,
Did my Mum live with that man
Right up until the time she died?

I think of her poor life,
I think of the tears that she cried.

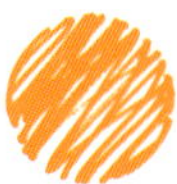

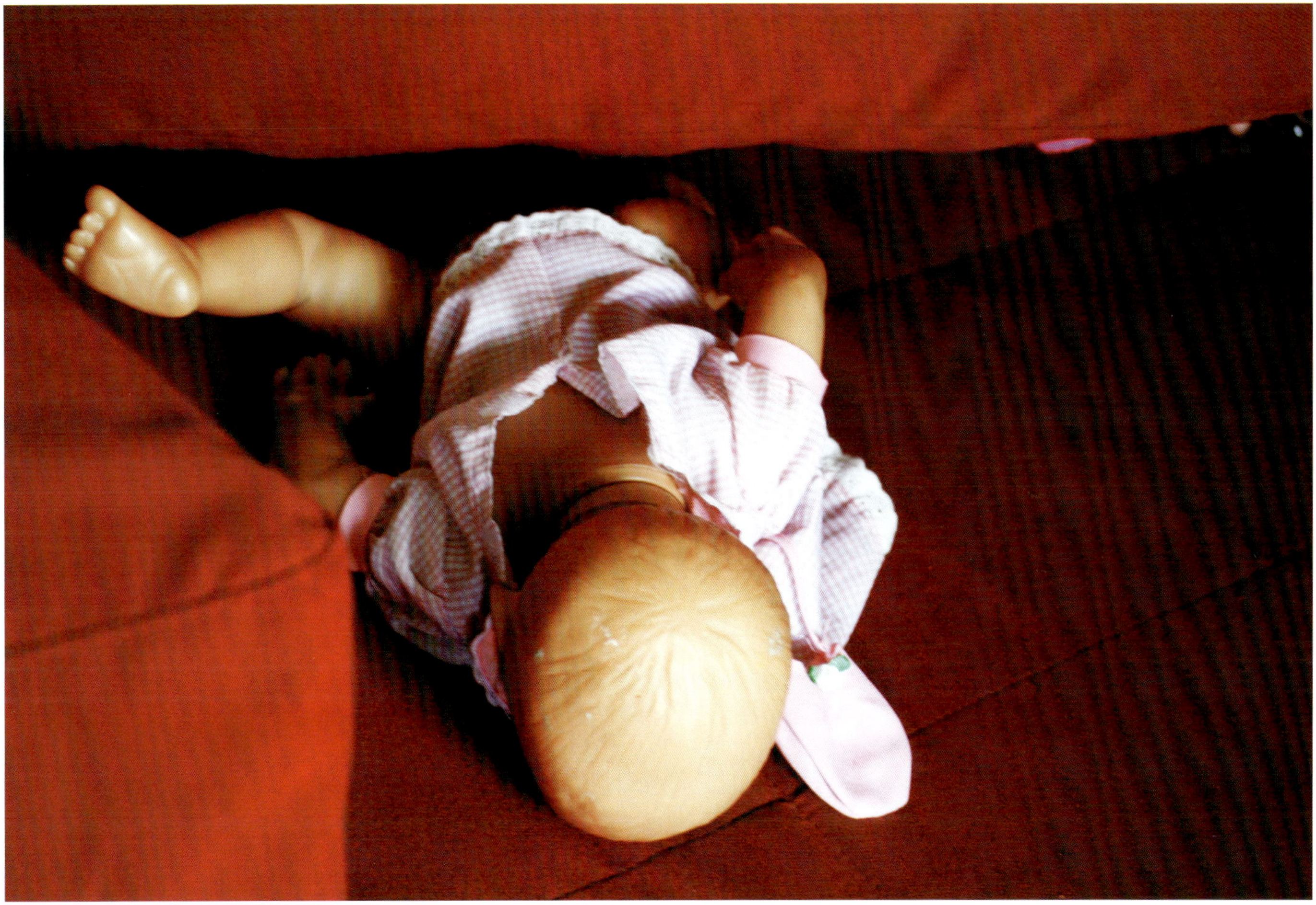

Graffiti on a Corner

Dermot Bolger

Each time I pause at this corner
 It unlocks a private code:
Myriad labyrinths of memories
 Flash past along the road.

The thrill of being chased, first kiss,
 First time to encounter love:
You may see a bare street corner,
 I glimpse a treasure trove.

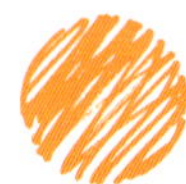

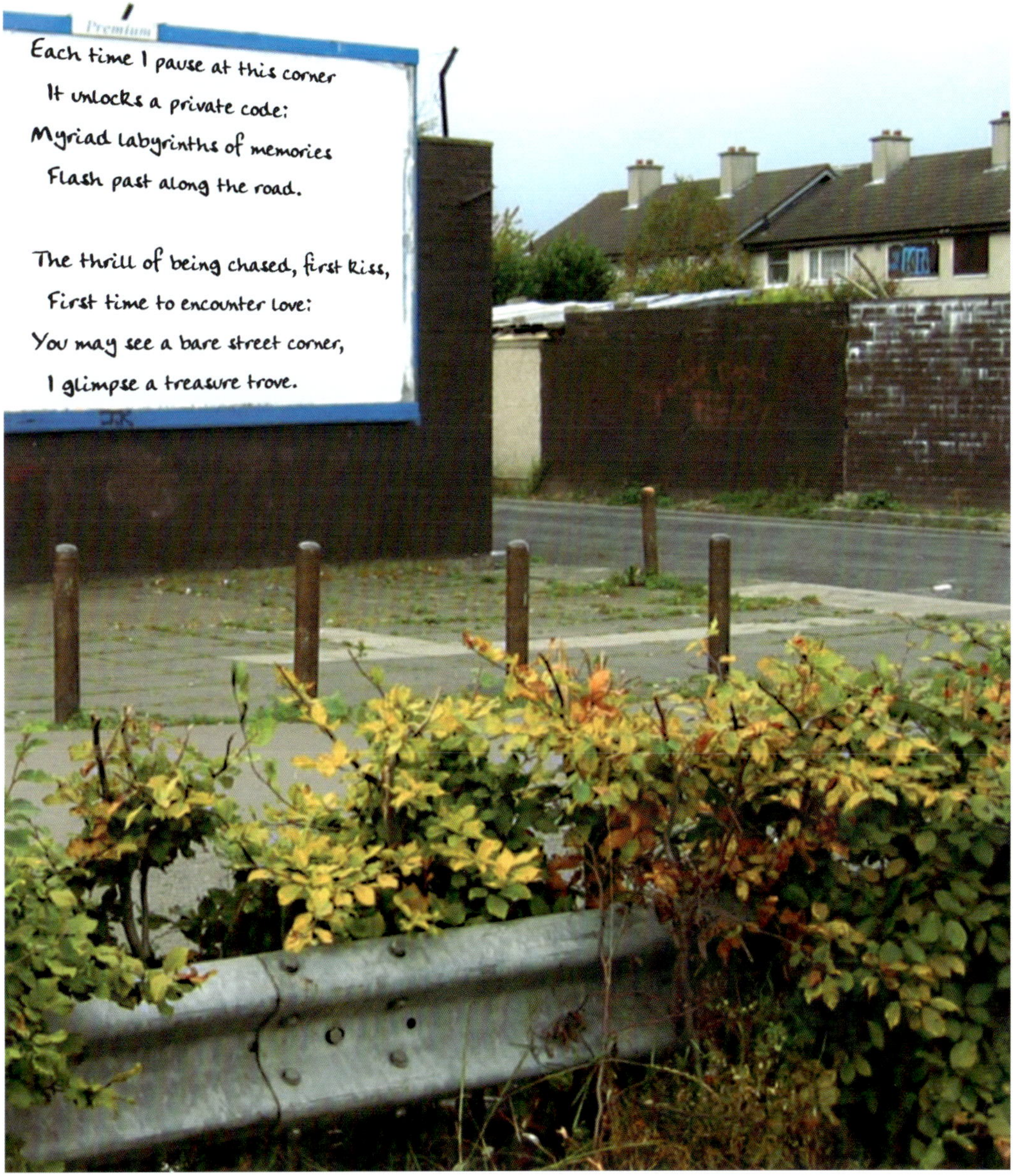

Each time I pause at this corner
It unlocks a private code:
Myriad labyrinths of memories
Flash past along the road.

The thrill of being chased, first kiss,
First time to encounter love:
You may see a bare street corner,
I glimpse a treasure trove.

The Pool

(The Back Drain, off the Grand Canal, Clondalkin)

Tony Higgins

I remember times
With sunburst energy
When I leapt
From sheets
To meet the day.

Disarrayed among the bushes,
Hung my clothes
As neat as
Storm tossed roses.
While, like a salmon lunging
For a higher pool,
I plunged
Into the stream.

Cold shock cold,
World beneath the water,
Sunlight kissed,
Grey rocks echeloned
To block the flow,
A small pool created,
We beavered with the dam.

A curious brown horse
Gives a brief
Five barred stare
Before departing, puzzled
By the din.

Now at crack of noon
I curse the fact
That I am forced
To confront
The slowly passing moments
That quickly total years.

Men of uncertain age
Talk kindly
Of those who died too young,
By chance or cancer,
Stroke or blade,
Retreating from life's high velocity,
Leaving small ripples on the pool.

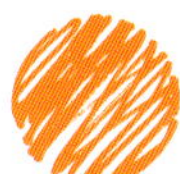

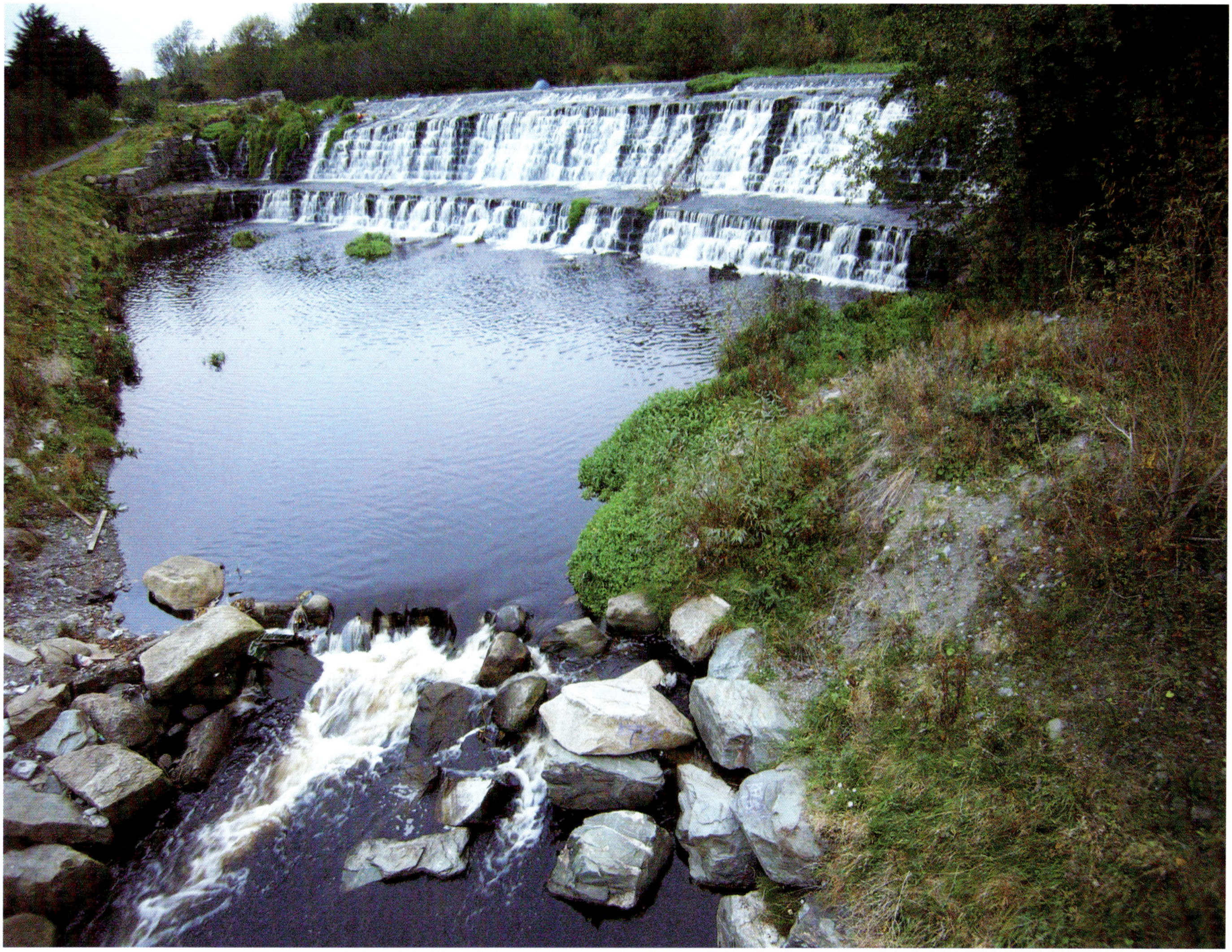

The Tallaght Tardis

(St Muirin's House, Avenbeg)

Aine Lyons

A grey concrete box,
Harsh, forlorn, almost Neolithic,
Huddled among the red-bricked
Brashness of new apartment blocks:
Yet inside astounding words are born.

Light floods the room as we fill
The circle of chairs and wait in wonder
For runes to dance, as one by one,
newly typed sheets of paper unfold.

Listening to the cadence of voices
Flooding our cave with a flicker of stars,
Tiny nebuli, soar on the updraft of stories,
Poetry flowing, as this surreal shelter
Becomes an aurora borealis.

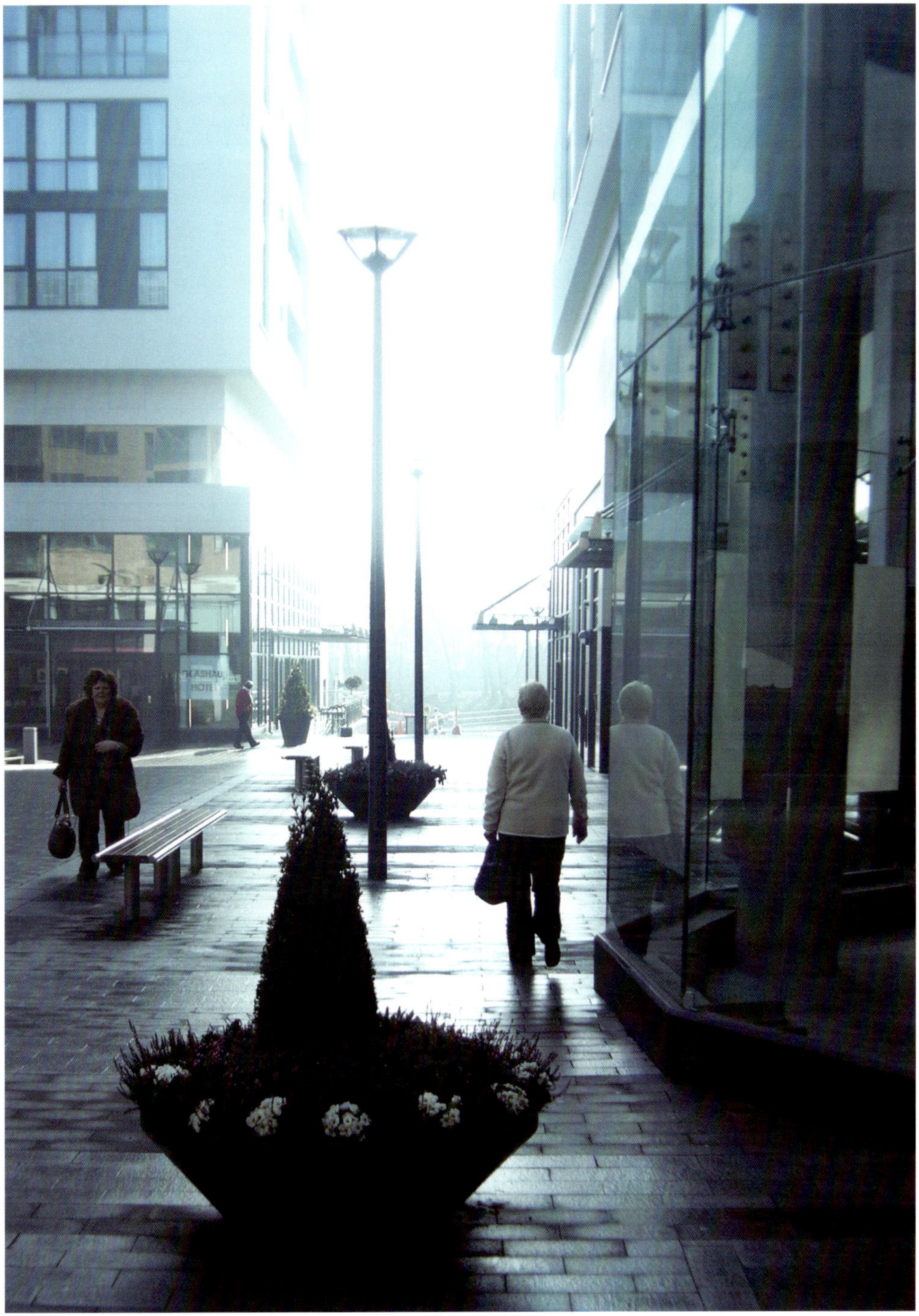

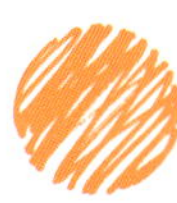

Passing Certain Estates

Dermot Bolger

On the night that they announce his death
Those of us who live in the homes he built
Will throng the gates that guard his mansion.

We will carry his oak coffin on our shoulders
In a silent procession through every estate
Where he ignored bylaws, left roads incomplete.

We shall dig a grave to half its legal depth
And lower his casket as far as it will fit,
Promising to return and complete the task.

His coffin shall be left jutting out on a slope,
And on his subsiding headstone will be writ:
"Death too has short cuts and sharp practices,
I lie as I left you, betrayed by empty promises."

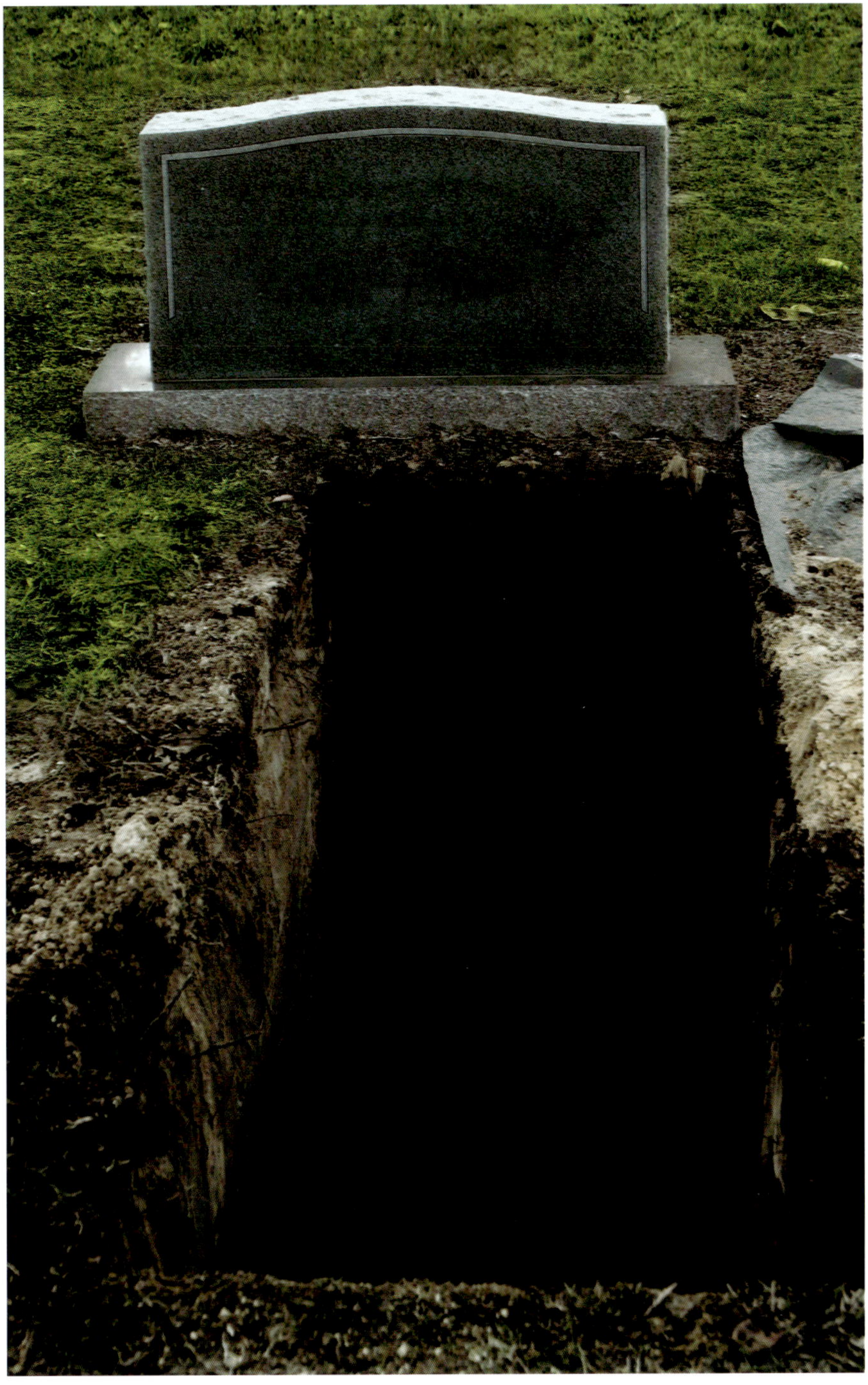

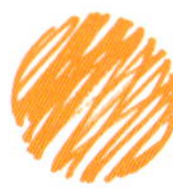

White Van-watching on Stocking Lane

Nessa O'Mahony

A secretive creature,
but increasingly seen
in fields and hedge-rows.
Nest-sites generally discovered
near planning notices tacked to walls
or sodden posts the wind has buffeted.

Mating habits unclear
as they are rarely seen in pairs,
though one was recently observed
bumper to bumper
with another, smaller variety
down the old road
to the dog pound.

Plumage invariably white
if mud-caked on the fender.
Some show the dents
of previous breeding.

Arrival heralds, not Spring,
but a definite change in season.
That field, clover-filled,
frilled by the red
of cock-pheasants,
soon transformed
by a rich swathe of cement,
the soothing thump of pile-drivers.

Happily, population numbers
give no cause for concern,
although we can never be complaisant
when it comes to wild life.

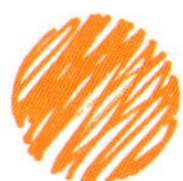

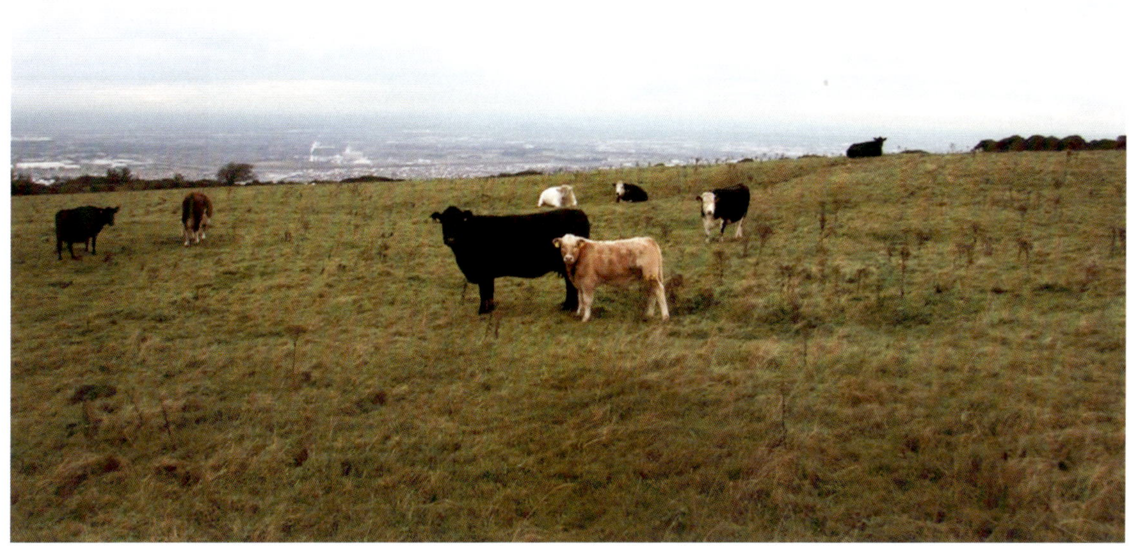

Great War Triptych

(Knocklyon House, Dublin, 1917 & 2007)

Dermot Bolger

1

Telegram boys were harbingers,
  Carriers of despair,
Bearing news of local boys barely
  Older than they were,
Down lanes in Ballyboden, Ballyroan,
  Whitechurch and Old Bawn:
Mothers in windows, transfixed to stone,
  Begging them to cycle on
Past their homes with the envelope
  Whose formulaic words
Extinguished the compulsive hope
  That was like an addiction,
As they beseeched God that the telegram
  Was about someone else's son.

11

These are the gates where the telegram boy stopped,
The window beneath which he crossed the gravel.
No sniper's bullet could be as loud as his knock.

Grief drifted in, shapeless as mustard gas, to linger
Along every muted corridor in Knocklyon House,
Sleet drummed against the slates like skeletal fingers.

The Great War spread from France and the Dardanalles
To requisition cottages in Tallaght and Rathfarnham,
Conscripting mothers once addicted to novenas

But now trapped in a No Man's Land of mourning.
A clock ticking off the infinity of empty afternoons,
A war against despair to be fought every morning

When it felt so easy to simply cave in and surrender.
The battlefront changes, yet a great war continues in rooms
Once filled with longing for a son missing in Flanders.

People wonder how they survived, having lost such friends,
How they will endure another night of ceaseless combat
Against desires that gnaw at arteries and nerve ends,

Against dark angels incessantly whispering in their minds,
That one drink, one hit, one bet, one click will do no harm,
How they will endure the void of leaving their fix behind.

111

Addicted people learn to cope, pacing corridors
  Where a dead boy's parents grieved:
Wounds raw, nerve ends jangling, desperate for
  Something that cannot be retrieved.
People who endured delirium tremors, endured detox,
  Suffered such symptoms of withdrawal
That they think they only imagine the elderly couple
  Quietly observing them in the hall,
Ghosts who survived, who came through anguish,
  Even if the yearning never retreated.

Knocklyon House in Knocklyon, Dublin, was the family home of a First World War soldier who died in the Ypres Salient in 1917 and whose body was never recovered. Today the house is used as the Rutland Centre for Addiction.

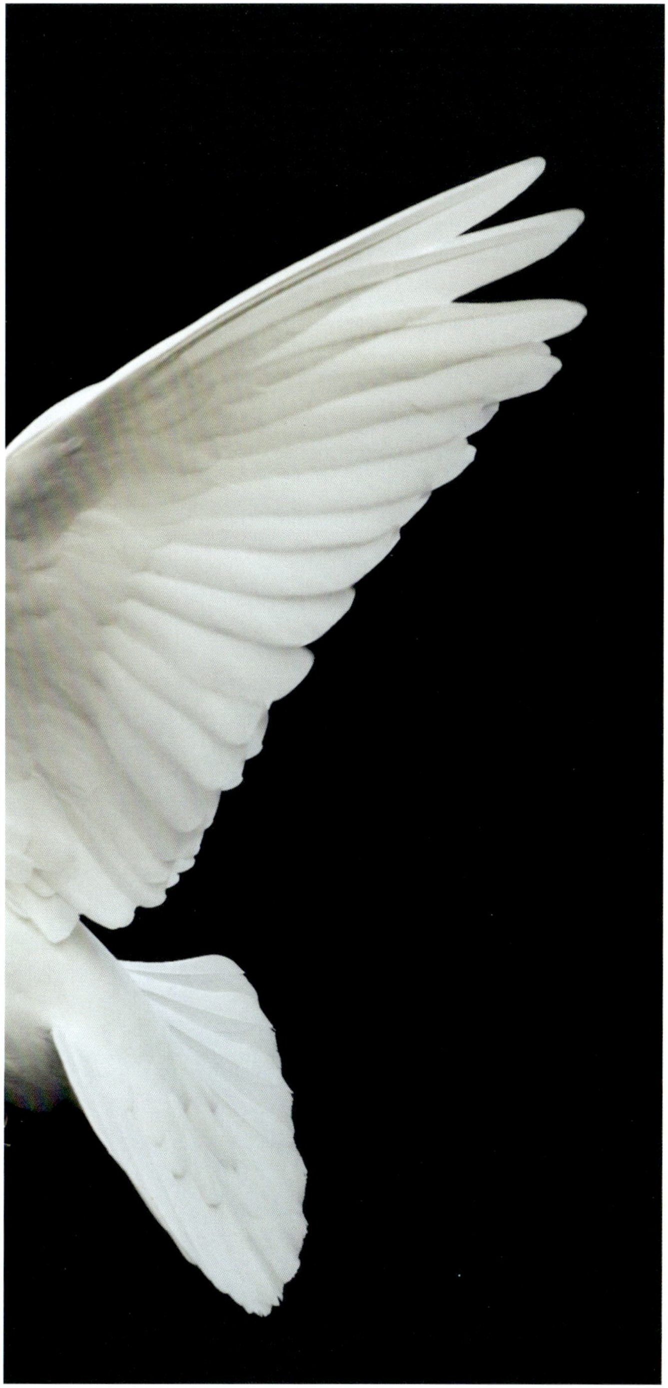

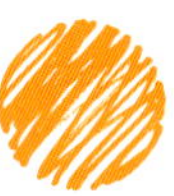

Rathfarnham Triptych

Padraig J Daly

1: MASSEYS' WOOD, IN THE LIGHT OF IRAQ

Even as I walk,
Watching for sudden showers,
Where bluebells spread infinitely
Under trees,
I grow aware of an elsewhere,

Where a man,
Erect and stricken,
Walks out
To lift his lifeless daughter
From a roadway.

11: MARLEY PARK

A swan today,
In a secluded corner of the lake,
Lifted its wings in the sun
Till the tips of its feathers
Disappeared in light;
It folded then its head
Into its downy breast,
Peeping slyly:

Reminding me of how bright sun
Plays colourgames with your hair as you race;
And then, the stop,
Remembering to be shy,
To find a skirt or pillow
To hide your face in
And peep at the attending world
With mirthful eye.

111: FIRST COMMUNIONS, BALLYBODEN 2007

Let the enchantment commence:

Deck the boys in slick suits,
Gel their hair.

Fit the girls out in petticoated frocks,
Pin cloth roses on their tresses.

Teach them to join hands,
Walk an aisle decorously.

Can it matter,
In God's enormity,

That few who watch,
Aglow in the light of a child,

Know the why of the bread,
Have any prayer but, "Thanks".

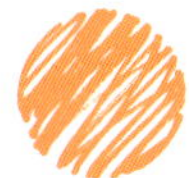

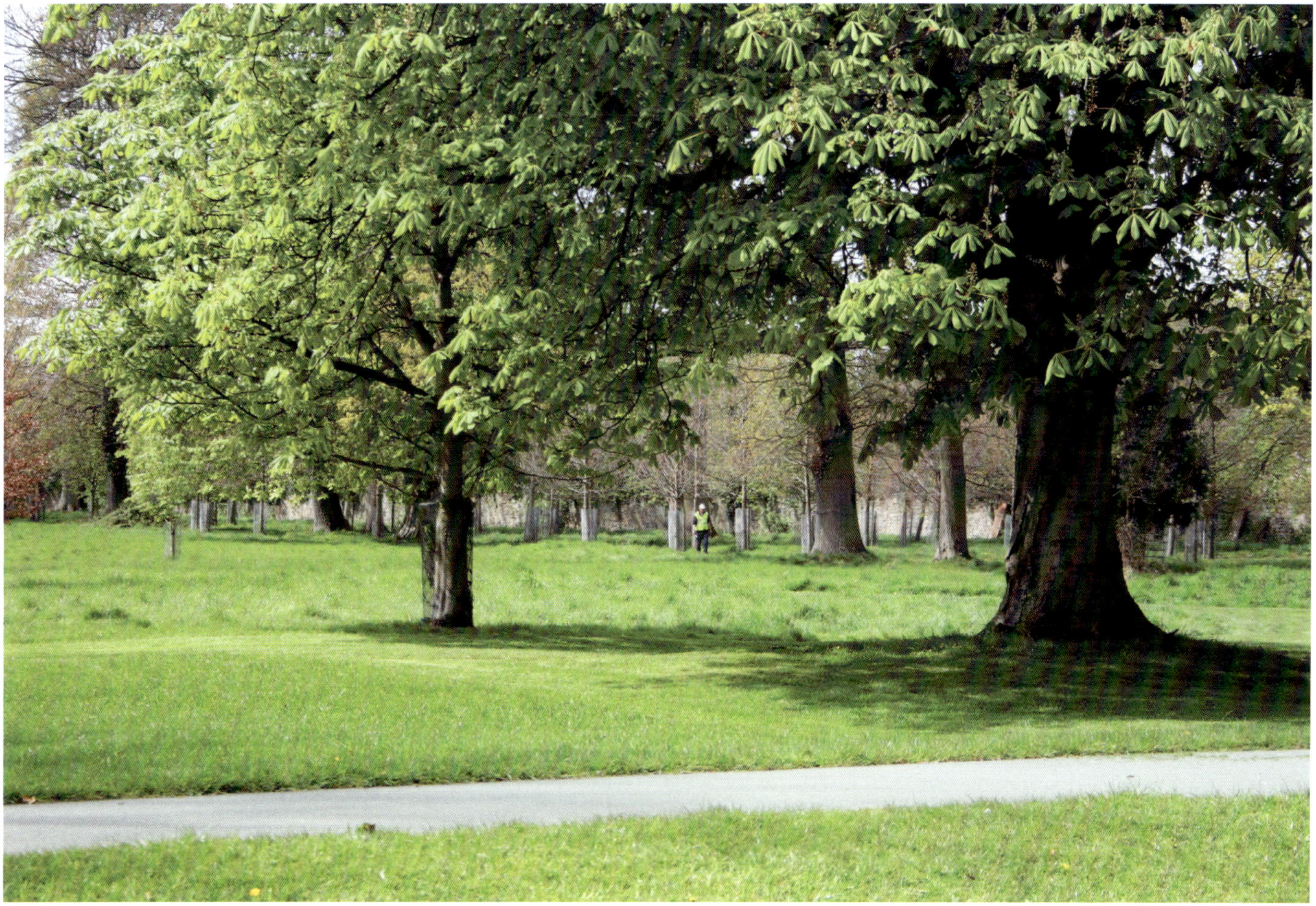

The Cut

Dermot Bolger

When the cut is decided four decades from now,
Should I prove to be the final golfer standing

I will leave for my friend a wooden tee neatly broken:
His Indian sign left behind to mark each perfect drive.

I will leave for my brother a ball miraculously perched
On the edge of an unplayable hazard, just within bounds,

Sitting up with such incongruous temptation in the rough
That some stranger cannot resist playing it when found.

For my brother-in-law I will leave a discarded cigarette butt
Nonchalantly smouldering on the fringe of a deserted green,

After being tossed away to allow him slay another par putt.

(Fourball, Edmondstown Golf Club, Rathfarmham
Founded by the Jewish Maccabean Society, 1944.)

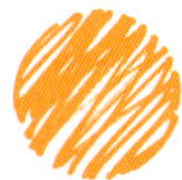

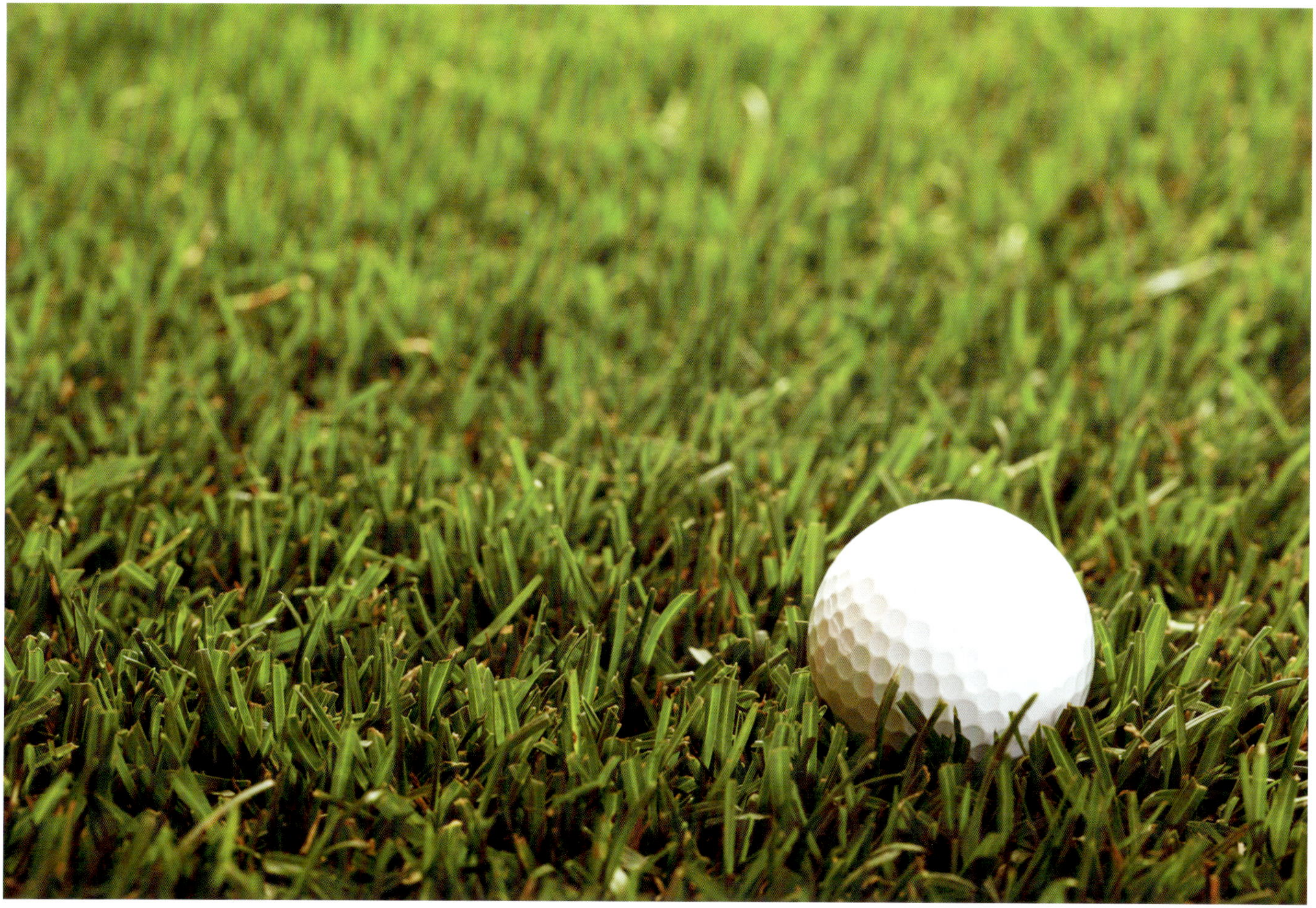

Holding His Hand

Colm McGlynn

Today we took a gentle stroll
From Rathfarnham Shopping Centre
To the post box in Templeogue village,

And Dad, in his 83rd year,
Became so jaded
I had to hold his hand.

Tears welled up in my heart
At this role reversal:

The man who held
My hand as a boy
Now in need of mine.

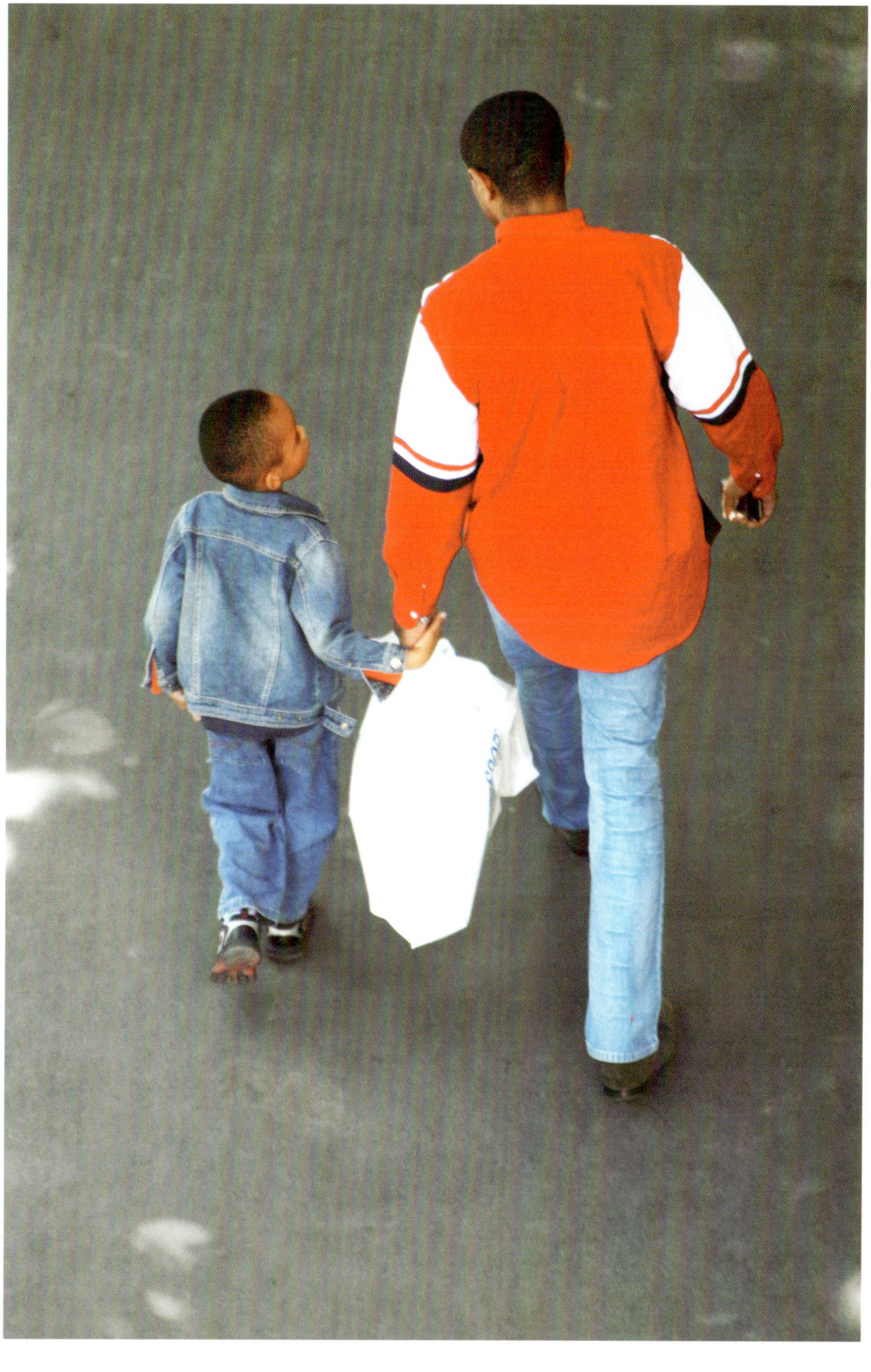

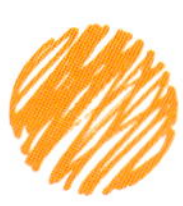

Gealt

Áine Ní Ghlinn

Léim gealt in airde ar bhus a sé déag inné
Agus pitseámaí air – stríocaí liath is dearg orthu!
Shuigh sé síos in aice le fear a raibh babhlaer agus *briefcase* air!
Rug an créatúr greim an duine bháite ar a *bhriefcase*!
Trí shuíochán síos uaidh chrosáil bean a cosa!
Rug máthair greim an duine bháite ar a páiste!
D'fhéach an páiste ar na ngealt!
Rinne an ghealt meangadh mór mantach gáire.

Labhair an tiománaí le fear an *depot*!
Labhair fear an *depot* le lucht 999!
Fuair sé lucht dóiteáin ar dtús is d'fhiafraigh siadsan de
An raibh an ghealt i mbaol nó tré thine nó in airde ar chrann?
Ní raibh!
Bhris an fear dóiteáin an líne!
Ghlan an tiománaí sruth allais dá éadan!
"A Chríost!" a scread sé – de chogar ar eagla go gcloisfeadh
Gealt na bpitseámaí é – "Cuir fios ar na *bloody* Gardaí"!

Tháinig na Gardaí is ghlanadar an bóthar amuigh i Rath Fhearnáin!
Tháinig an t-arm is luíodar taobh thiar dá leoraithe, meaisínghunnaí
crochta!
Tháinig na dochtúirí lena gcuid steallairí is le veist cheangail…
Tháinig an bus!
Bhí fear an *bhriefcase* báite ina chuid allais féin!
Bhí bríste an tiománaí fliuch!
Bhí bean na gcos crosáilte fós coschrosáilte!
Bhí rúnaí a bhí le bheith in oifig mhór i Sráid Chamden
Leathuair a'chloig ó shin anois i Rath Fhearnáin!

Bhí an páiste ag stánadh ar an ngealt!
Bhí an ghealt ag súgradh le cnaipí a phitseámaí
- é fós ag gáire go mantach!
… Stad an bus!
… D'ardaigh an ghealt a cheann!
D'aithin sé dochtúir!
D'aithin an veist cheangail!
Is é fós ag gáire léim sé suas is rith amach an doras
Isteach i lámha an dochtúra!
Isteach sa veist a bhí gan lámha!

Istigh sa bhus phléasc osna faoisimh!
Níor labhair ach an páiste
"A Mhamaí, cén fáth nach ligfeá domsa mo phitseámaí
A chaitheamh ar an mbus?

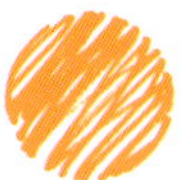

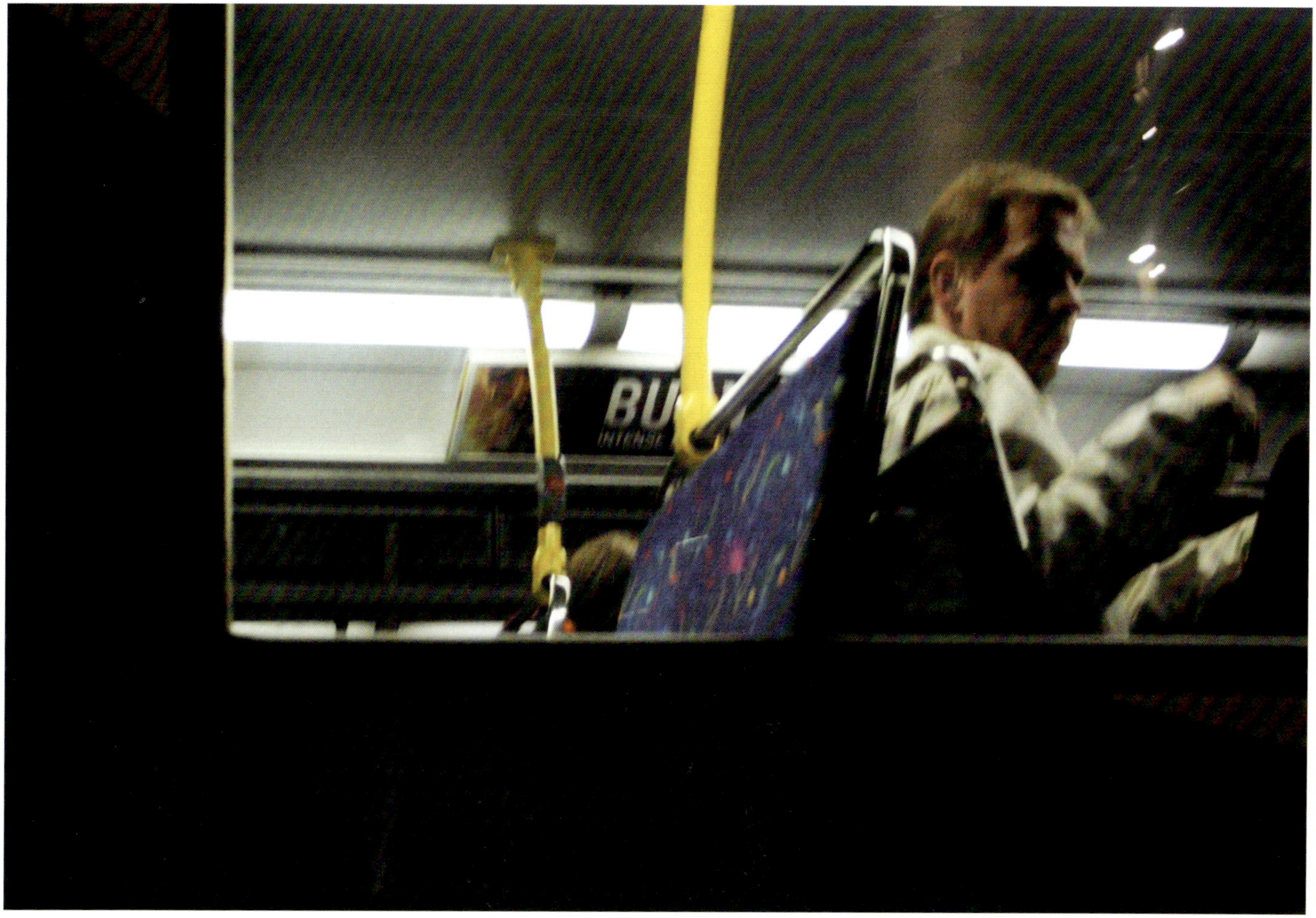

Evening

Take A Haiku Home

Joan Power

As the light declines
Rough cradling of Dublin Bus
Rocks me homeward bound

Nest mate flown ahead
We'll roost upon our millstone
Crowing with relief

Dawn will catapult
Reluctant cogs of commerce
City bound once more

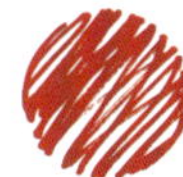

Conquistador, Pilgrim Soul

Dermot Bolger

Three times I have sacrificed myself as a martyr,
Given up my life so that others might escape,

Three times this week I was betrayed by daybreak,
Three times I rose again to reboot my computer.

This is my life, or dare I say, my true existence.
Their world of enduring eight hours in an office

Before queuing twice a week in this evening traffic
To study in the Tallaght IT, no longer feels realistic.

Reality only starts when I arrive home to my duplex,
To dine with a plate placed in front of the screen,

When I anticipate the unknowns that may occur,
When I decide what universe I intend to inhabit,

When I prepare to play games against strangers
And to off-load real estate in my cyber abode.

In the IT they think me peculiar, call me a loner,
But I am far from alone. A world-wide web of us

Refuse to recognise their restrictions and borders
On who we are and who we are allowed become.

I know where I belong and it is not amid this traffic.
Like my grandmother, I believe in another existence,

But while she filled her heaven with plastercast saints
I populate mine with sinners, fantasists and dissidents.

My parents believe in nothing but the news on television.
"You're twenty-four", they say, *"you know nothing yet."*

But I know that their universe is the ultimate illusion,
With everything rationalised and carefully packaged

And all eventualities covered by an insurance plan.
Anyone can find me in my world and yet no one can,

There are no lanes cordoned off by traffic cones
But infinite space to be whoever I decide that I am.

I have personalised my private version of heaven:
It resonates with mythic beings, living and dead.

I know my visitors only as whom they claim to be.
Perhaps the driver opposite me in this tailback

Visited my site last night pretending to be a girl?
Maybe that is his reality, made flesh in one click?

Perhaps only the lies we concoct are actually true,
Because we select them by our own free choice:

Our true skin colour, true sex and true voice.
I was given no say in my nationality or birth,

But in cyberspace I make these choices myself,
Floating free of restrictions imposed on earth.

At the screen I can become my own creator,
I can discover the true core of my soul,

There I can become all the parts of myself,
Indivisible at last, finally made whole.

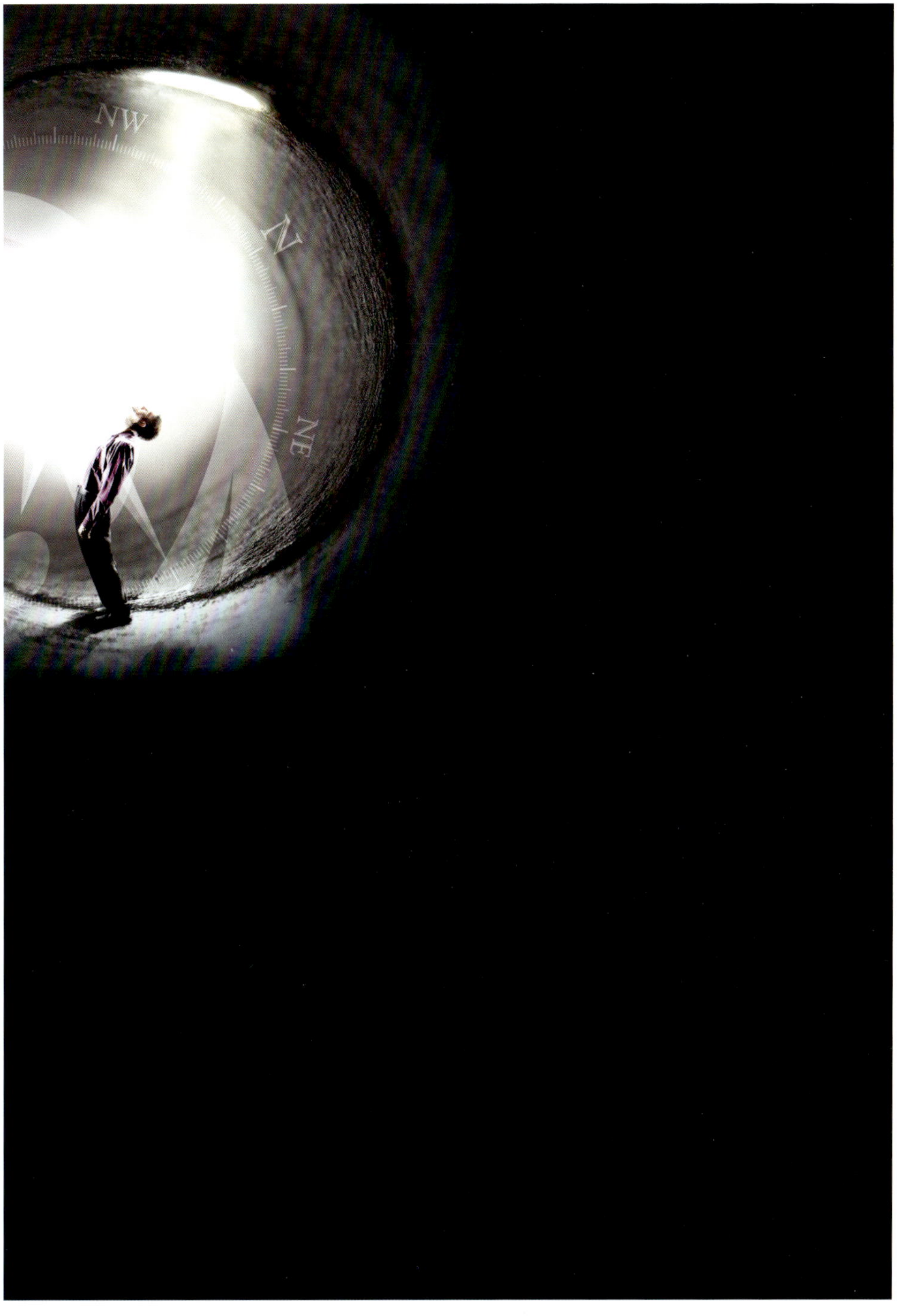

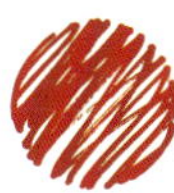

Reflections

Betty Keogh

Through the window
Their features look familiar,
Yet I don't understand their tongue.

Luas stop after stop
People board and alight,
Dusk turns into dark.

We whiz past streetlights:
Factories, houses, the Square,
Apartments climbing skyward.

I feel like a foreigner
In my native land.

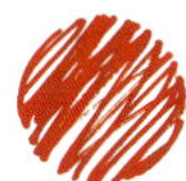

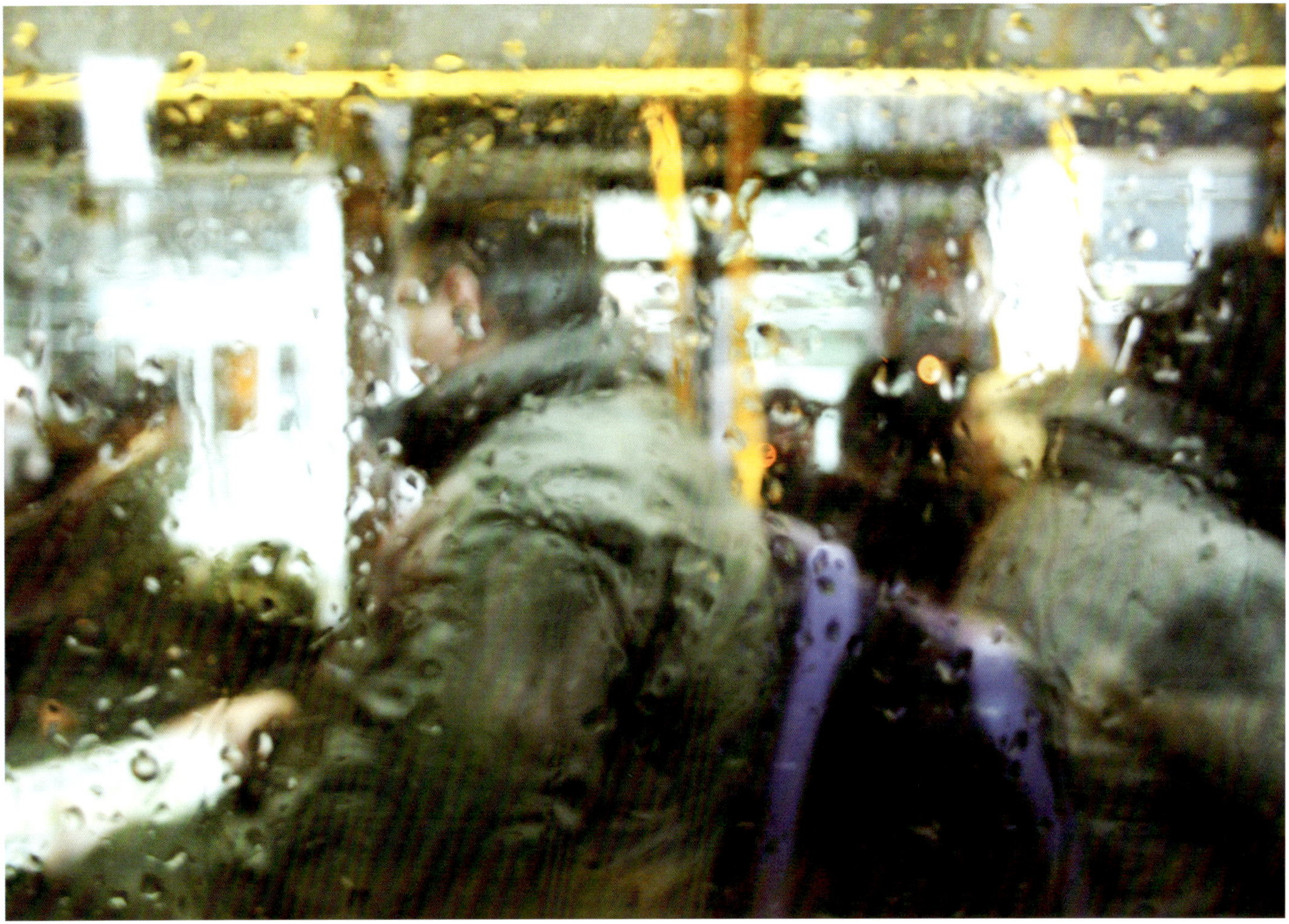

Wedded

(For Bernie)

Dermot Bolger

This is what I am wedded to:
The bus journey in the dusk,
Tailbacks, roadworks, queues,
Tired faces staring into space
Thrown forward in our seats
As the driver applies the brakes,
Intrusive glimpses into lives
As strangers chat on phones.

The name carved on a boulder
At the entrance to our estate,
The sweep of curving rooftops,
The bicycles left on the path,
Hopscotch marked out in chalk.

The light in the kitchen window
When she gets home before me,
The bustle of pots, the radio
Blathering about the outside world,
A scent of spices as she says hello,
Busy stirring a dish at the stove.

The voice of the woman I wed,
Who makes every aspect blessed,
This kitchen, this suburban street,
This bus trip like a pilgrimage
Back to where I may finally lie
With my bride amid shoals of roofs,
Amid the vast galaxies of estates,
Amid the myriad specks of light,
In the place where I am safe,
Where I wake deep in the night
And touch her sleeping face.

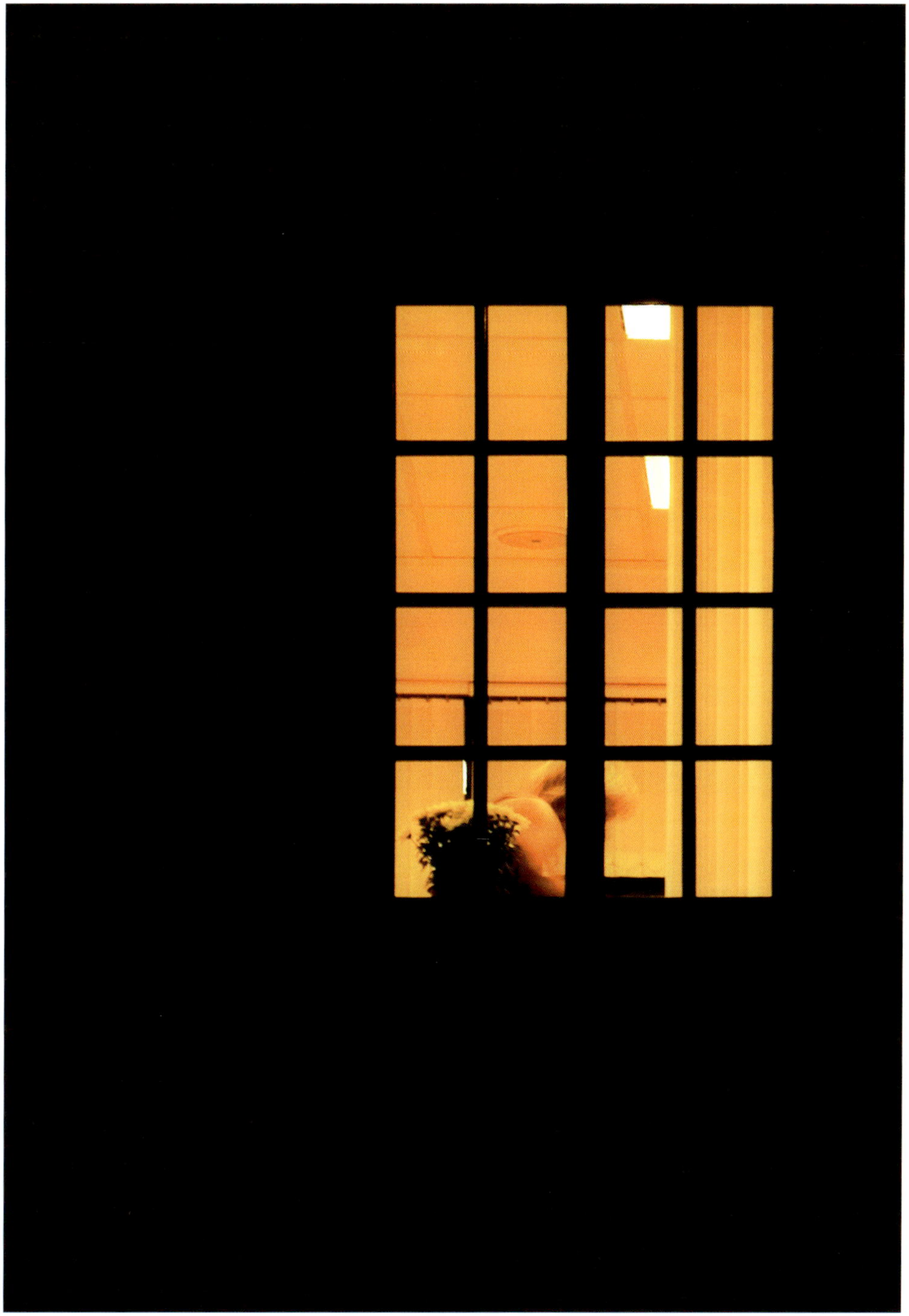

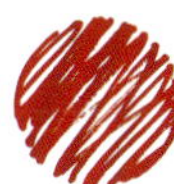

Kilnamanagh Triptych

Gerard Smyth

1: Housewarming

For luck we brought a nugget of coal
and salt: the double talisman
to protect our four walls and fire-hearth.
The on-off switch bestowed electric light
that was all yours, all mine, all we had.

We were ankle-deep in builder's rubble,
dwellers of a bare house,
hammering nails and sweeping the dust,
making the space around us feel like home.

Bare wood cracked like knuckle-bone
when we crossed the floors
or climbed the stairs to take our places
side by side in the last sliver of dusk,
the first rays of the sun.

2: One Evening After Songs of Praise

It was our first home, built on ground
that belonged to ghosts,
on a height that in January caught the first snows,
that in June came alive when it became
a place for outings on golden evenings,
for *hide-and-seek* and *finders keepers.*

The house settled, absorbed new sounds:
a stereo playing *New Kid in Town,*
the easeful kettle coming to the boil,
banging doors, the rattle of cups,
our firstborn speaking first words in his high chair.

One evening after *Songs of Praise*
I stepped out into the cul-de-sac,
lifted my gaze
and saw the lights come on in upper windows,
the glow of televisions.
Out of the dusk fragrance, the eerie calm,
a voice called the names of children lingering
in one last game of *catch-me-if-you-can.*

3: Everyday Life

The heart-sighs of letters gust
through the letter-box.
Our children on the doorstep chant farewell
- together they are going back to books
that lead them forward. Wintersmoke
broods over the rooftops.

Effortlessly all morning the dissonance
of the kitchen grows:
a radio tosses rock music on the table,
the washing machine jolts its giddy load.

The housebound silence of the spare room
is rooted to serenity.
Embers of the moon form an eerie ghost-moon
making a leisurely, late departure.

A breeze that shakes and quivers
brushes the smell of sleep
from pillowslips on the line.
You think you can hear the trickle
of a stream, but it's water in the downpipe,
rain that falls a second time.

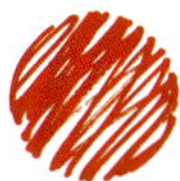

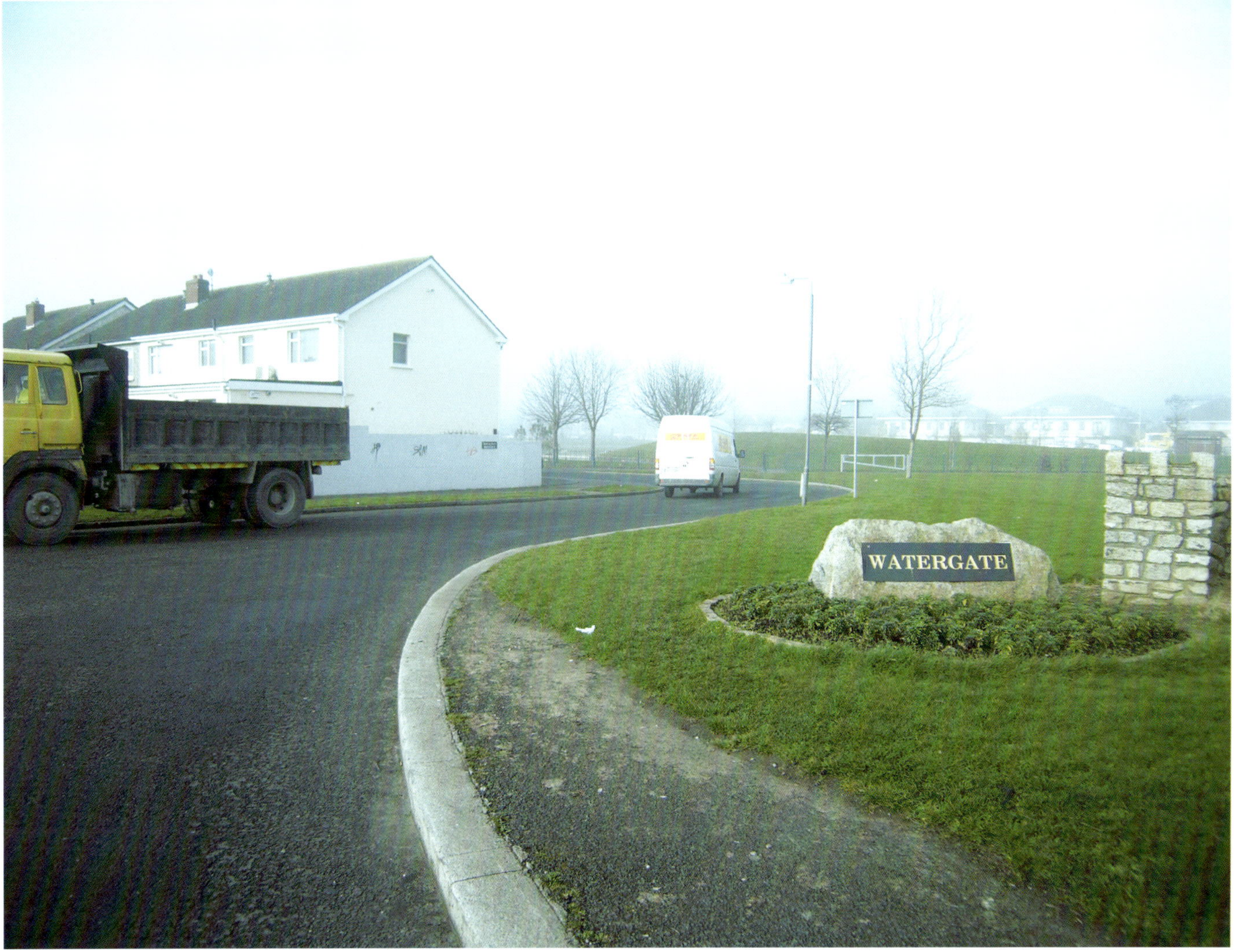

Silent couple in a red car, leaving Old Bawn

Dermot Bolger

I no longer know how to try and recapture
The intimacy which once existed between us,

So harmoniously woven that we barely noticed
The coded rituals of touch holding us together.

One night we forgot to close the fridge door
And by morning a small transparent glacier

Had enveloped our kitchen, edging upstairs
So that we woke inside an ice-capped world.

We remain the same people, except that now
We can watch every breath we take harden

Like a slow spectre formed by ectoplasm
In this arctic atmosphere. I feel scared

Because once you said that you could not live
Here on this earth without me by your side,

But each breath shows you no longer depend
On my love to exist. If I died you would survive,

Because you are ready to step from our capsule
Amid the rooftop galaxies, too absorbed to notice

My hands banging against the small glass porthole
As you cut the cord, drifting free into the universe.

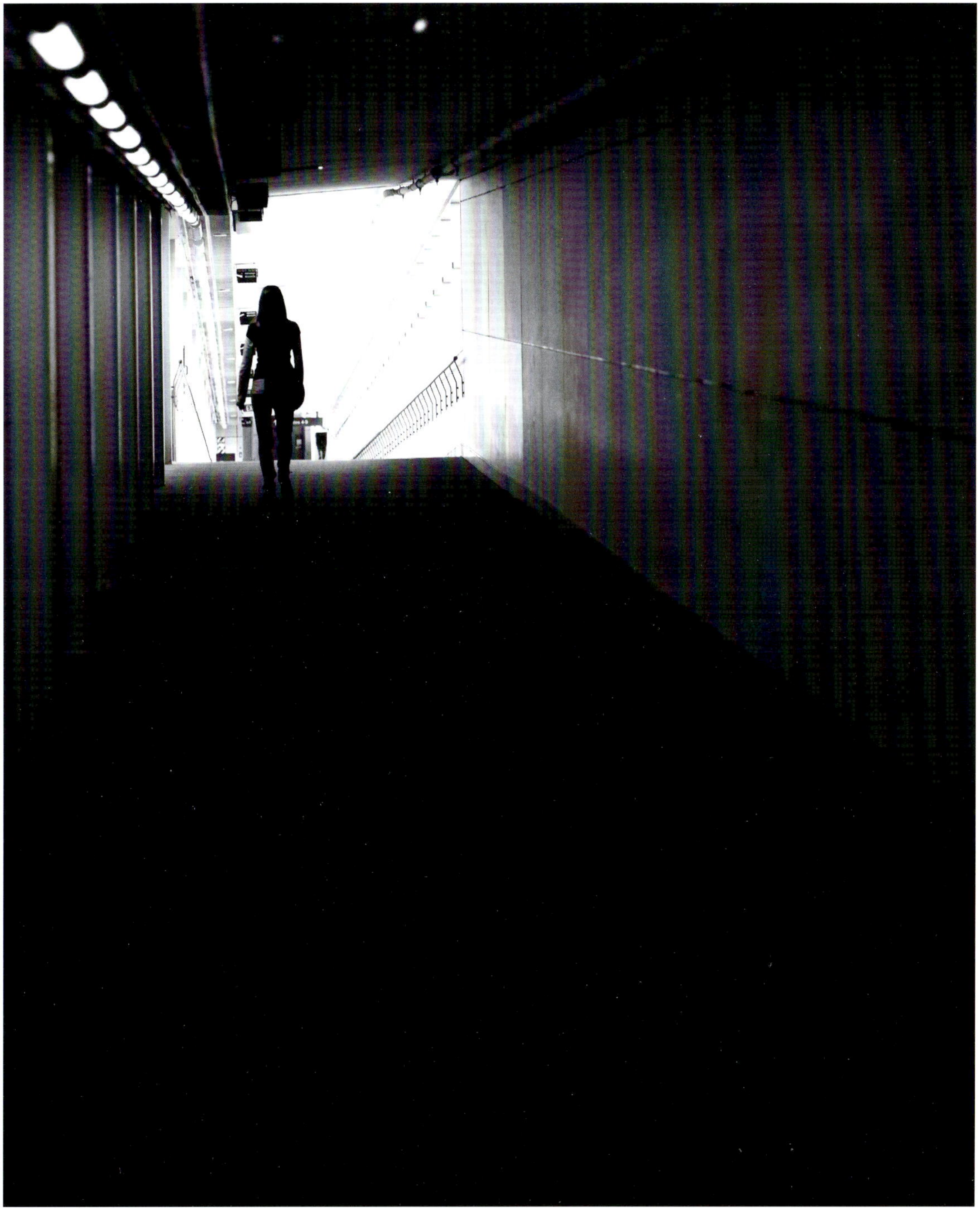

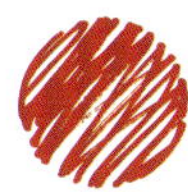

Quiet

David Mohan

It's easy now. We've been practising
For years, you and I. We started noisy,
Decorating, sitting on bricks in our garden,
Or shouting our love in the night.

After a while we forgot
The sounds of the world,
And the sound of the other's voice.
We adopted silence
In place of a child.

Now I store words in quiet,
On the sly, imagining
I've put *'softly'* in a muffled drawer,
Or hidden *'discreet'* between the sheets.

I make *'happiness'*
Shimmer in a teacup.
I bury *'passion'*
In the long grass of our garden.

At dinner I mouth *'delicious'*
So you don't notice.

Now I listen for the creak
At the gate that marks
The end of everything;
Now you come in
And hang up your coat,
And shake off your boots,
And give me the look
That kills the words in my mouth.

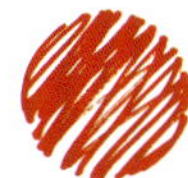

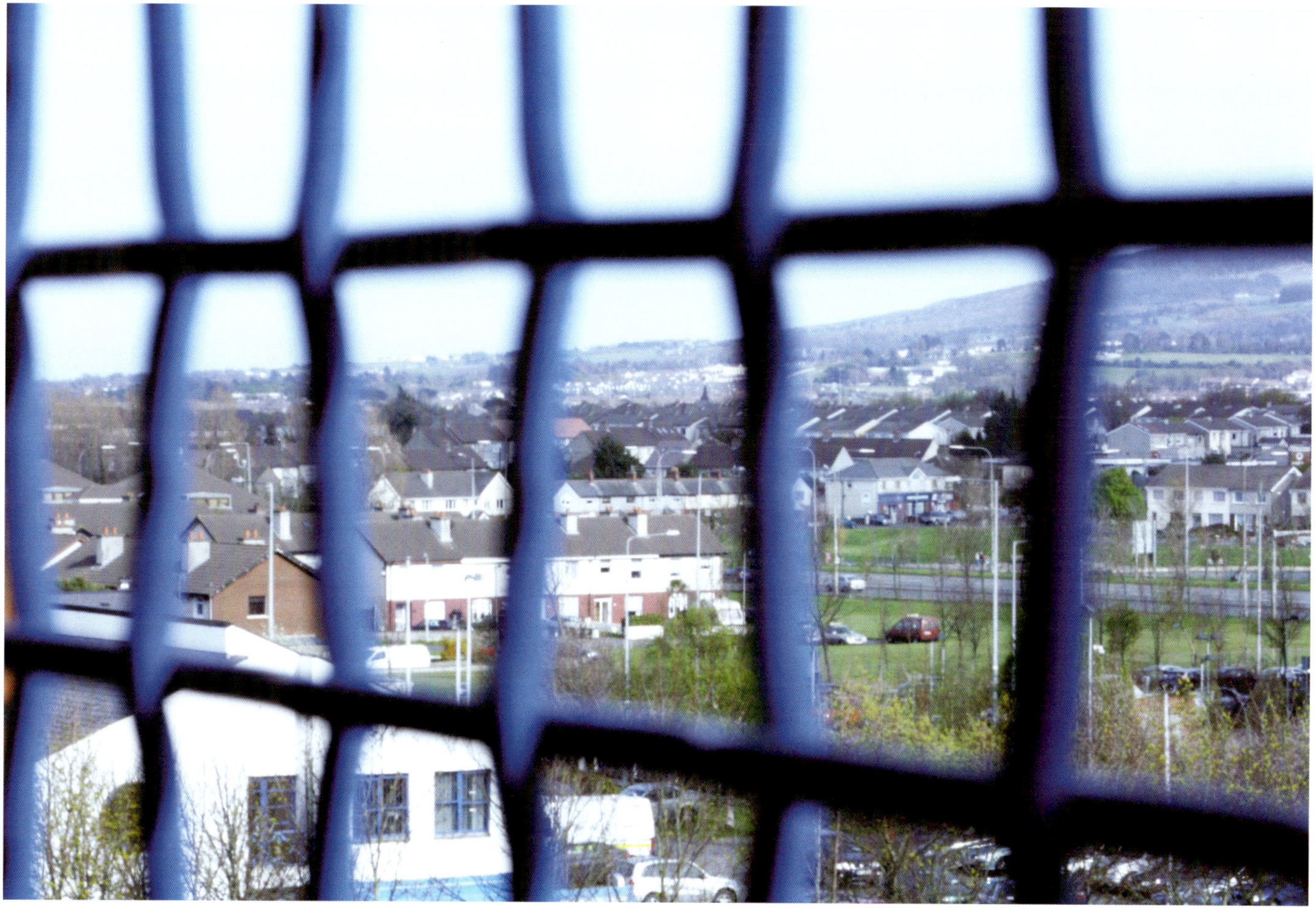

The Absent Fathers

Dermot Bolger

I am the smiling man letting go his hand at the door,
Timing to the last second when I must bring him back.

I am the six days of purgatory when I torture myself
With longing for a glimpse of his eight-year-old face.

I am a succession of happy meals and playgrounds,
An opened wallet, a question he cannot express,

An extra portion of fries, a man trying not to obsess
About making each moment we spend together count.

I am the cause of confusion, I am a boundless love,
I am a blemish in what should be his fairytale world.

I am the father who only catches glimpses into his life,
I am a monthly standing order, a hunter with his gun

Who lost his way out hunting, a sailor adrift at sea
Outside a Clondalkin house, meekly awaiting my turn.

I am a weekly routine, a slot allotted by a mediator,
A concerned voice unable to discern if he is all right,

I am the name that he has learnt not to call out for:
The absence who cannot banish his fears at night.

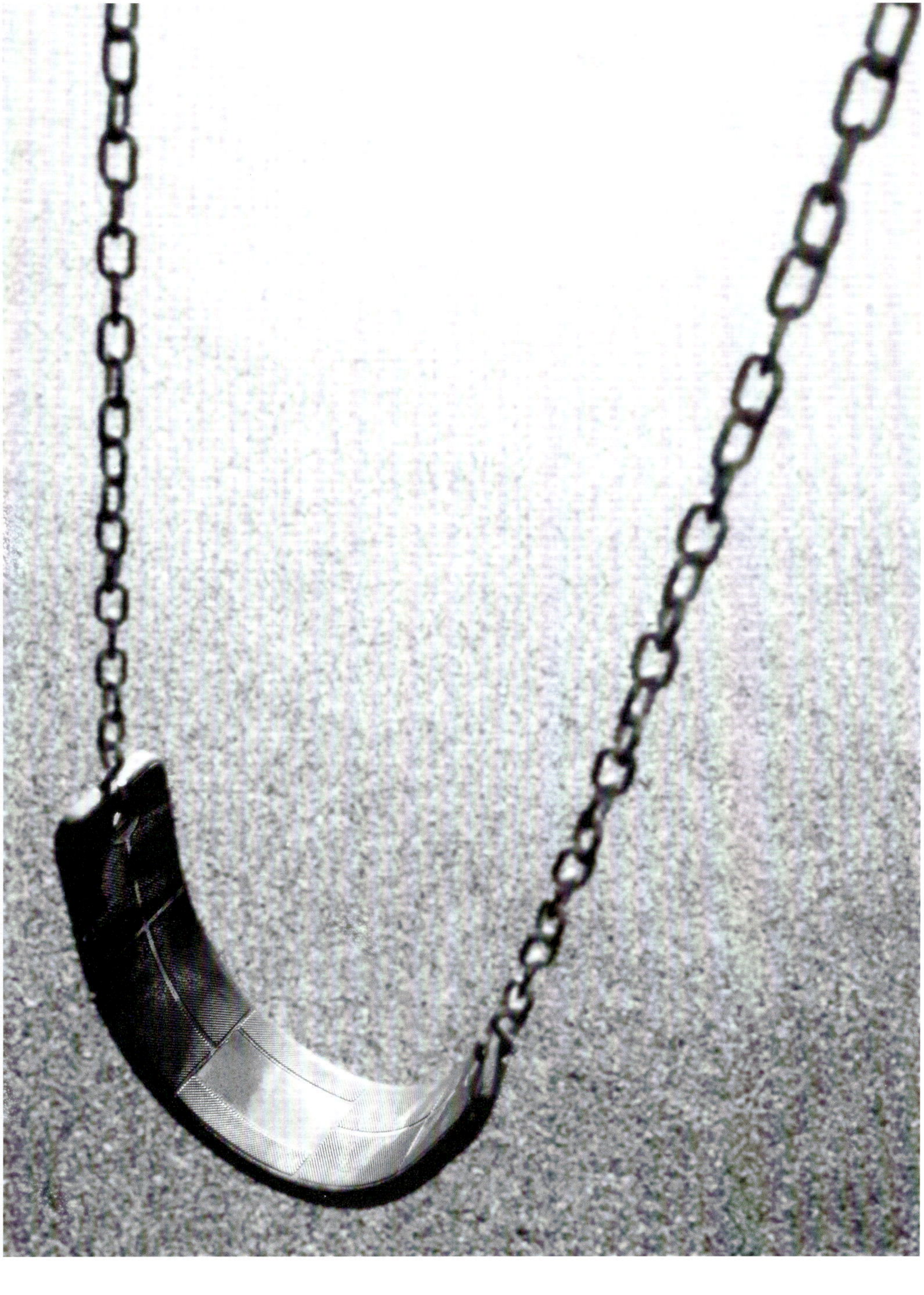

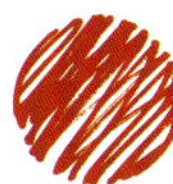

An Irish Suburban Love-Song

Kevin Power

The world is hardly smoothed with honey
For those whose burden is their money.
When all you've got is banked and filed,
And when your life is perfume-mild,
The time will come when you'll discover
It isn't easy to recover
From the plastic surgeon's knife
A sense of what you want from life;
And southside lawns in summer glory
Won't suggest a larger story –
They'll merely tell you who you are
According to your brand of car.

But what the hell did you expect?
You *made* yourself be circumspect.
You always did what you were told.
And now that you are almost old,
You sing the song that you heard sung:
"I made the right decisions young."

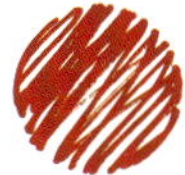

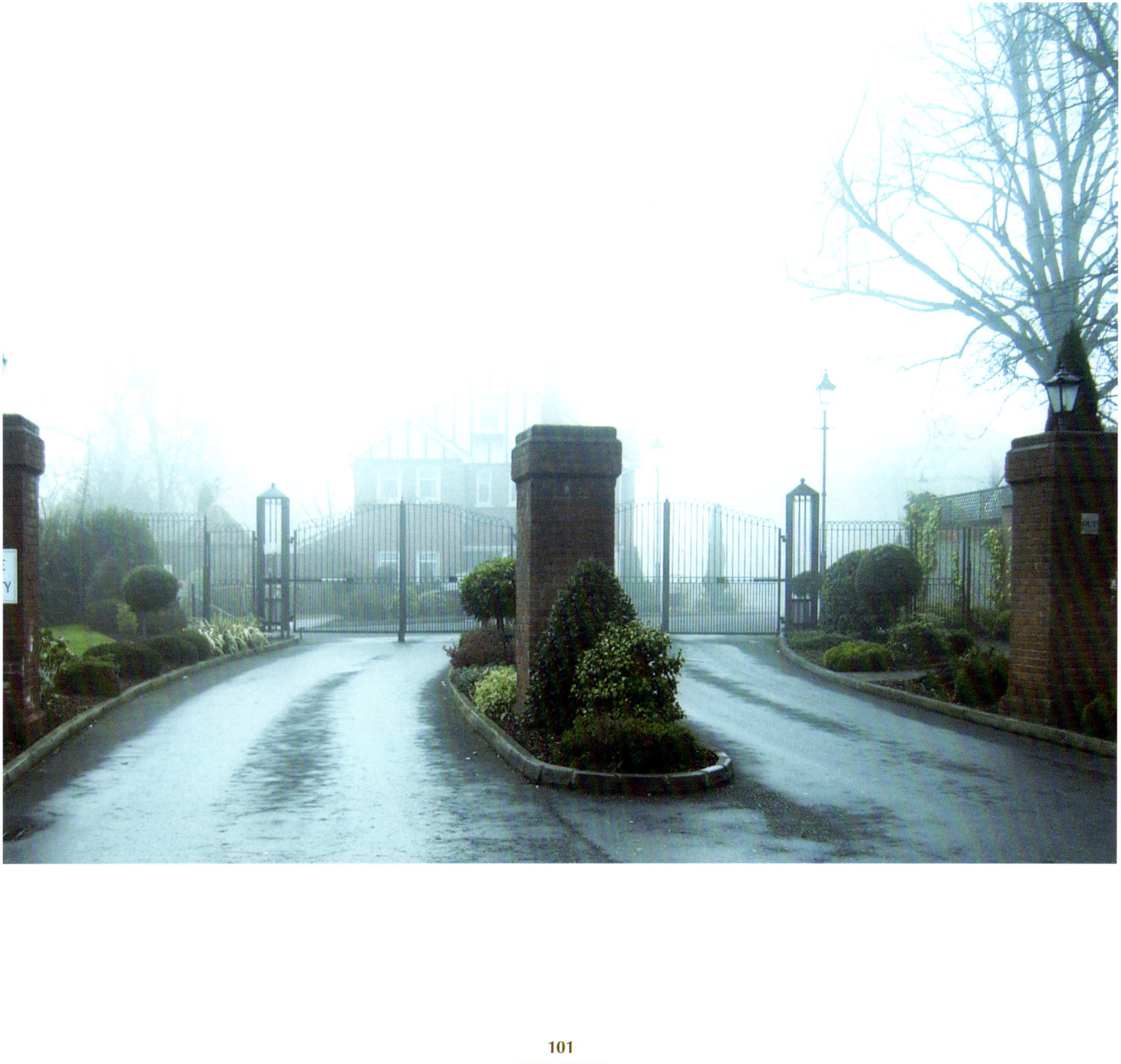

Night

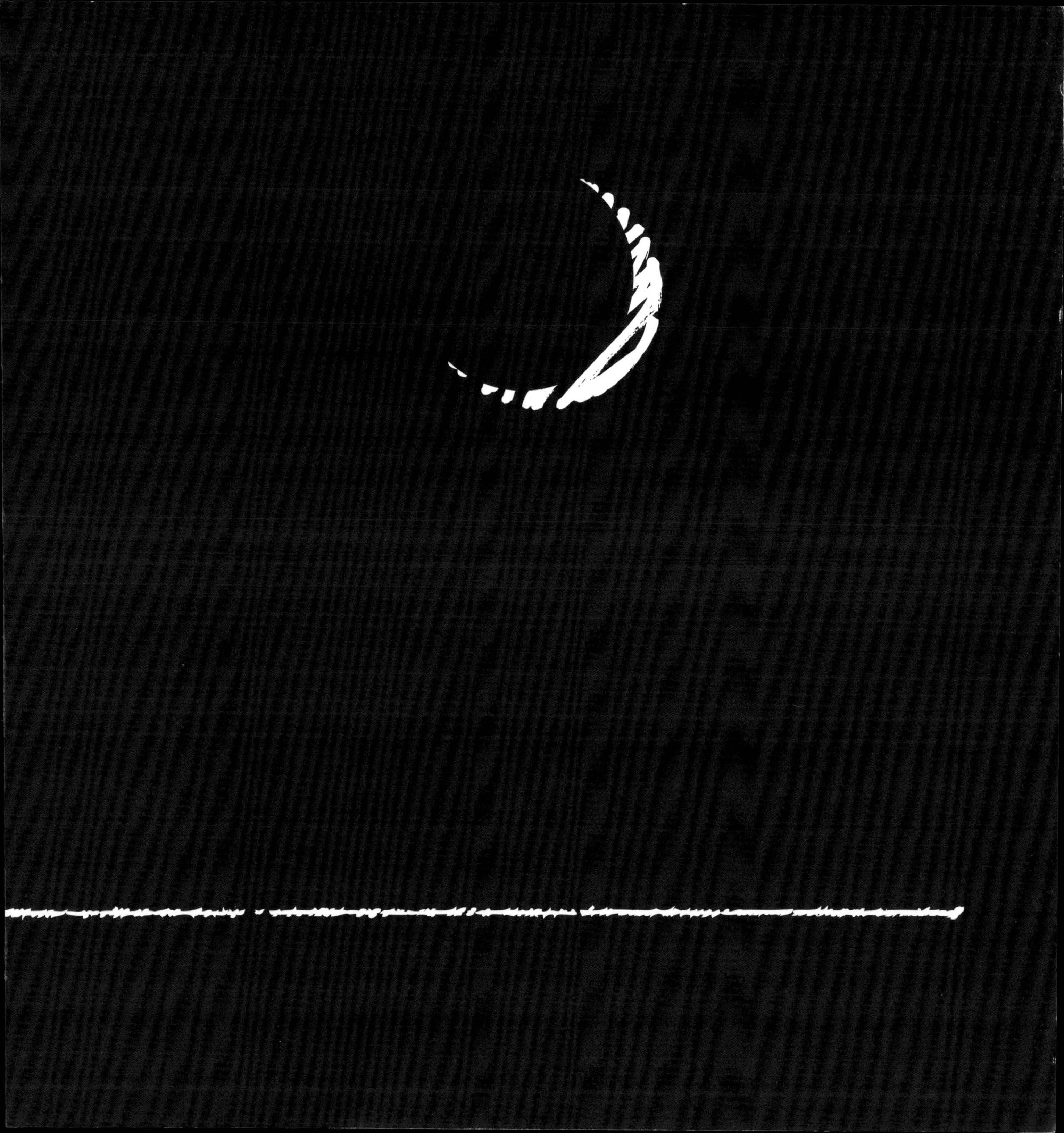

Things He Will Miss...

Dermot Bolger

His son growing in time to look like him;
The way that his girlfriend's face will age;

How they will finish building Clondalkin;
How other racers' memories of him will fade

Until his name becomes a mere postscript,
With younger drivers oblivious to his feats

As they video each other turning doughnuts,
Cocooned behind tinted glass and sun strips.

How the buzz fades from woofers and wheelspins
When one night you cease to feel indestructible;

How sons are meant to shoulder their parents' coffins
Not leave them to shoulder the ache of absence.

He will miss his son playing football in the park,
Cadging cash for dates, slagging his music tastes.

He will miss hearing the boy drive off into the dark,
The purgatory of night hours spent lying awake.

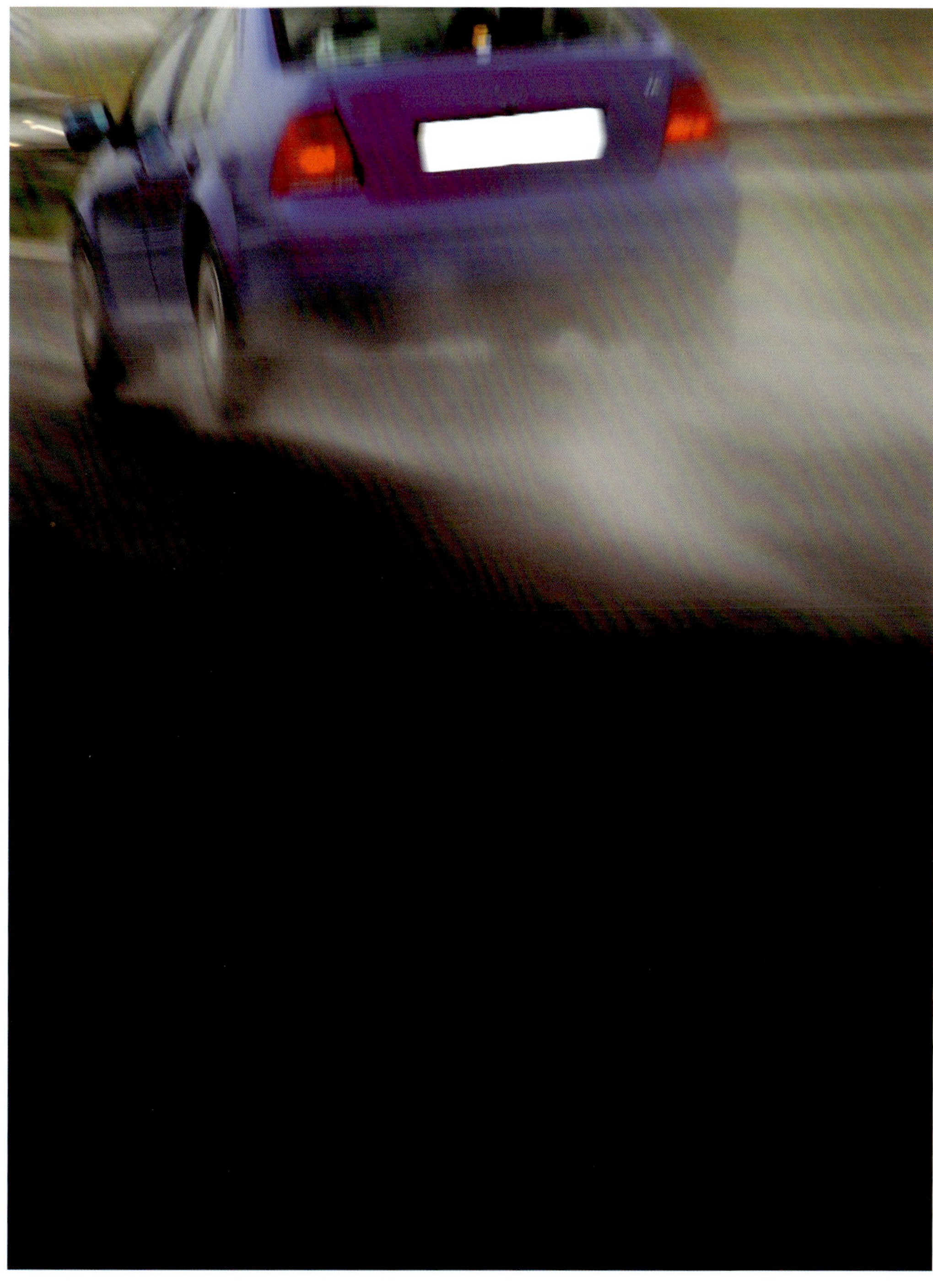

Dear Dealer

Colm Keegan

Don't get me wrong:
I've had nice times with blokes like you.
Been in the company of some real nice joes.
Young bucks with bright clothes,
Dudes, buds and bros
Who brighten a room with their presence.

But it is endlessly depressing
When you lean in close like that
And say 'Listen - If you're stuck,
I'll hook you up:
I've Coke or blow,
Just so you know'.
And the way you wink,
Not realising what I'm thinking

Like, are you stupid or what?
Or have you simply forgotten
All the other scurrying specimens?
Yeah, sure,
You'll be different,
You're going to make it:
You'll avoid the rats on the run,
All the psychos with guns

And if you do survive
you'll end up just like the rest,
Making the common man's worst nightmare
Your twisted best

You'll develop a blindspot
For the children watching
When you shoot men in the head.
All hopscotch stopped dead
By some bro or Daddy's blood
Spraying a short spattering rain
That burns like acid
Into their childhoods.

But no, not you:
Hands open, you plead
Your one of the nice dealers,
You'll just take what you need
You have nothing to do with the bodies piling up in newspapers
Filling my front page for what feels like forever,
Brains exposed to the air,
A heaving mess of black thoughts and goo
To be tiptoed around
And waded through,
Not just by me
But by every other poor shmoe
Who lives in this coliseum
That your greedy claws
Have the gall
To maul and shape
From the muck on our once clean streets.

So please, excuse me
If for the sake of my dignity
I will keep you away from me
And in my mind paint you black,
As I smile with quiet tact
And count the targets on your back as you leave.

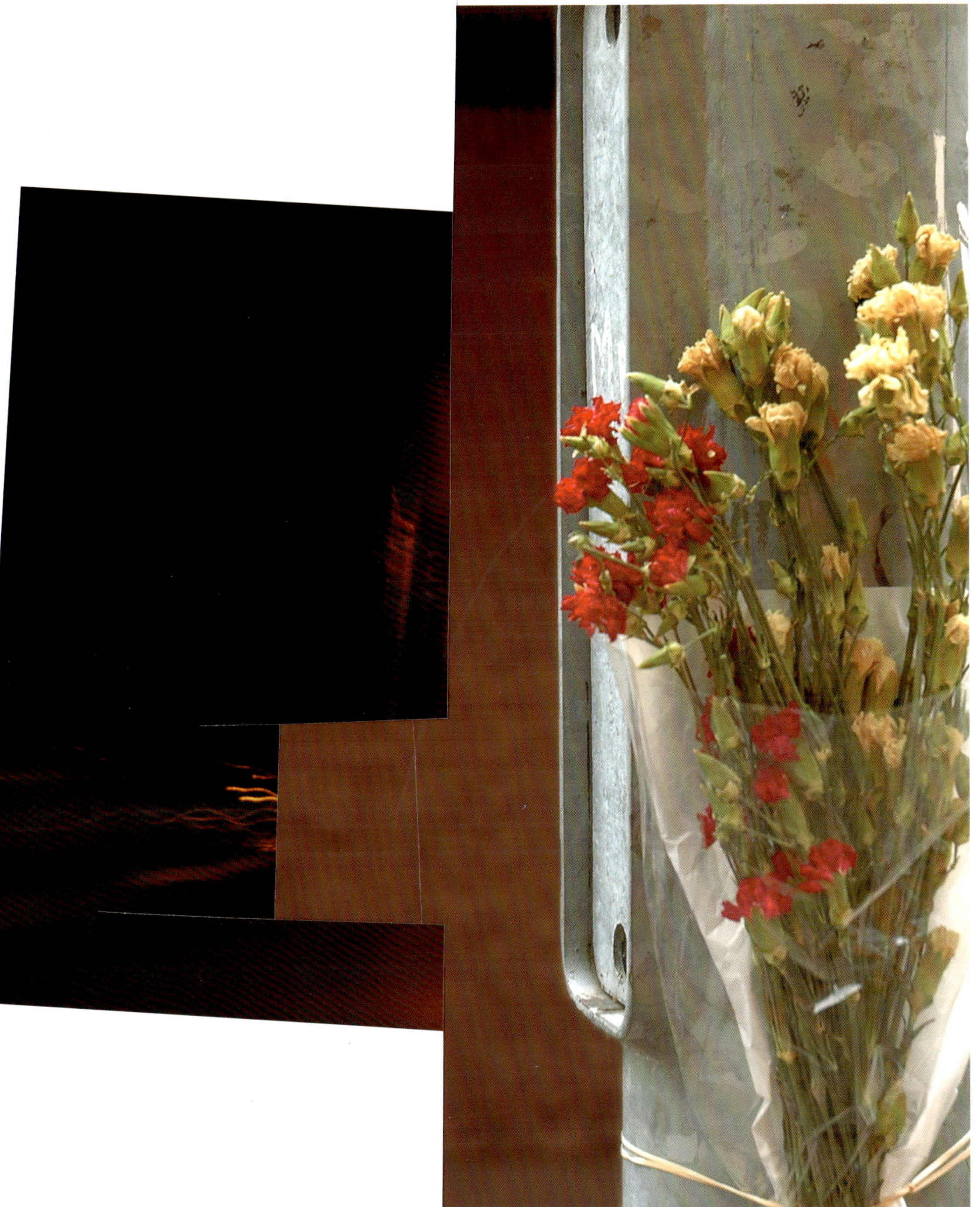

Two Weeks Before Night

(Maguire Ward, Tallaght hospital)

Maria Wallace

the girls make a fuss,
flutter around him:
how did you do that?
They laugh watching
his swift hands in which red kerchiefs
appear, coins disappear.
What about a bird? one asks.

Some other time. Perhaps.

The nurses, barely out of their teens,
tease and humour a handsome
forty-something man.
No birds? They entreat,
connect his oxygen,
know the impossibility
of certain things,
even for a magician.

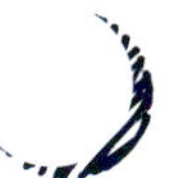

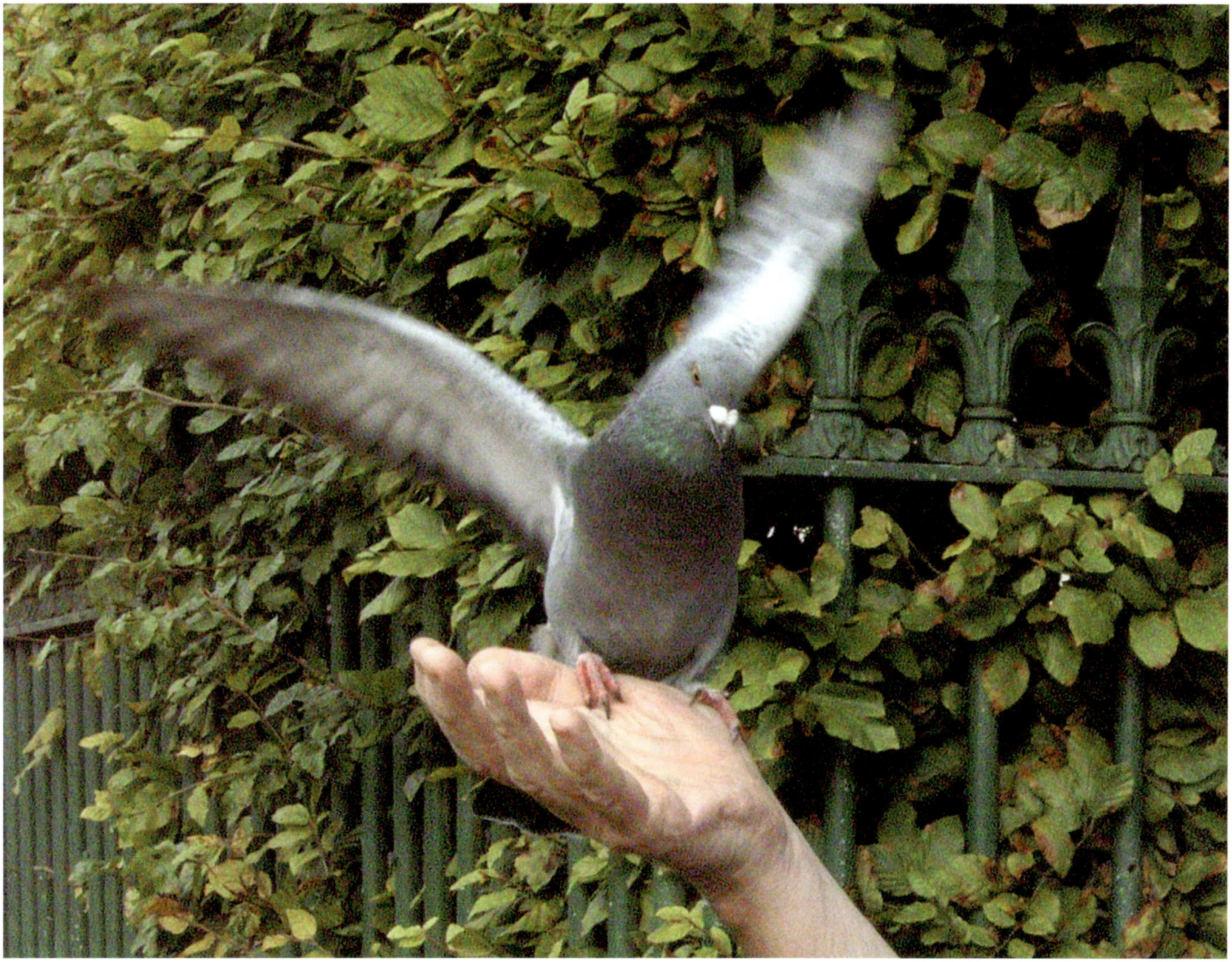

Haulier passing The Red Cow Roundabout, 11.15pm

Dermot Bolger

I just want to be home, is that too much to ask?

Even when asleep I see white lines, hard shoulders,
Automated cranes on foreign wharves loading ships,

I see that final container that I still have to deliver,
The one that always seems to keep me from home,

I see tailbacks and blockades and upturned wreckage,
Docksides where I smoke when sleep refuses to come.

The blonde teenage hiker incessantly pulling a comb
Through her hair as she climbed up into my truck,

Strung out on heroin, falling asleep on my shoulder
With the same smile as my thirteen-year-old daughter.

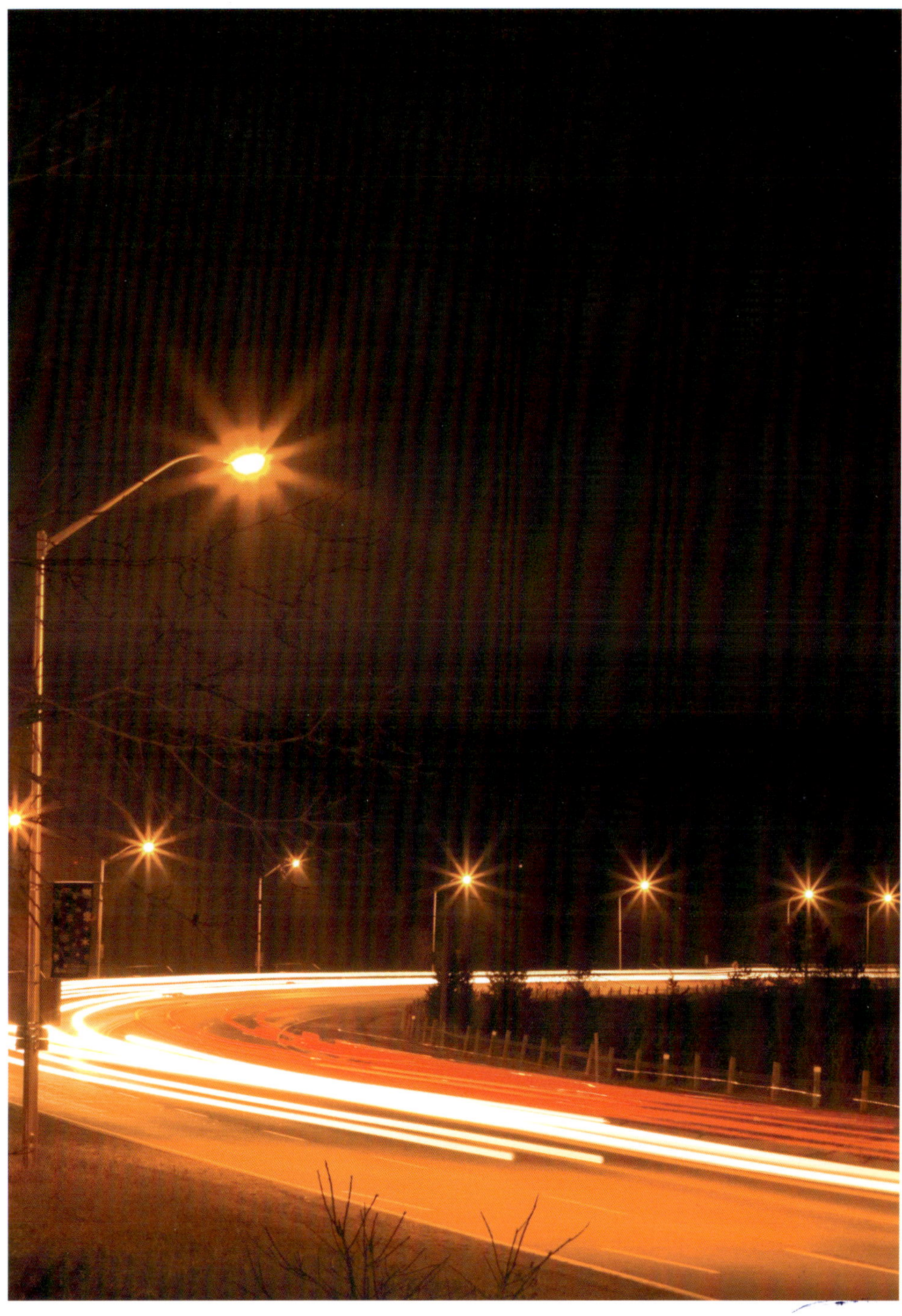

Secret lives of the Dodder

Muireann Allen

In limp half light the badger's twisted body
Can be glimpsed
Tossed in the grey green undergrowth
Eyes staring, still stunned
From the unexpected bang
Delivering him back on to the bank.

His body lies surrounded by empty beer cans,
Discarded plastic cups. The river winds
Around dark woodlands, this suburban park.
Ancient trees that stretch bare branches
Against navy skies hang like giant cobwebs.
A willow weeps, bends graceful over the river,
Whispers to the rush of water over stones.

A shopping trolley is perched
At the river's edge
its metal bars glinting
In the street lamp overhead.
The river flows on
Past houses where soft glows from bedroom windows
Give the first signs of stirring life.
On it rushes, tumbles under the old stone bridge
Where a lonely figure sits hunched,
Cigarette in hand. He picks himself up
Starts to shuffle away into the shadows,
The glowing embers of a fire
The only evidence that he was here.

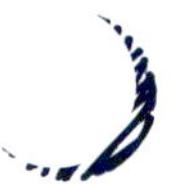

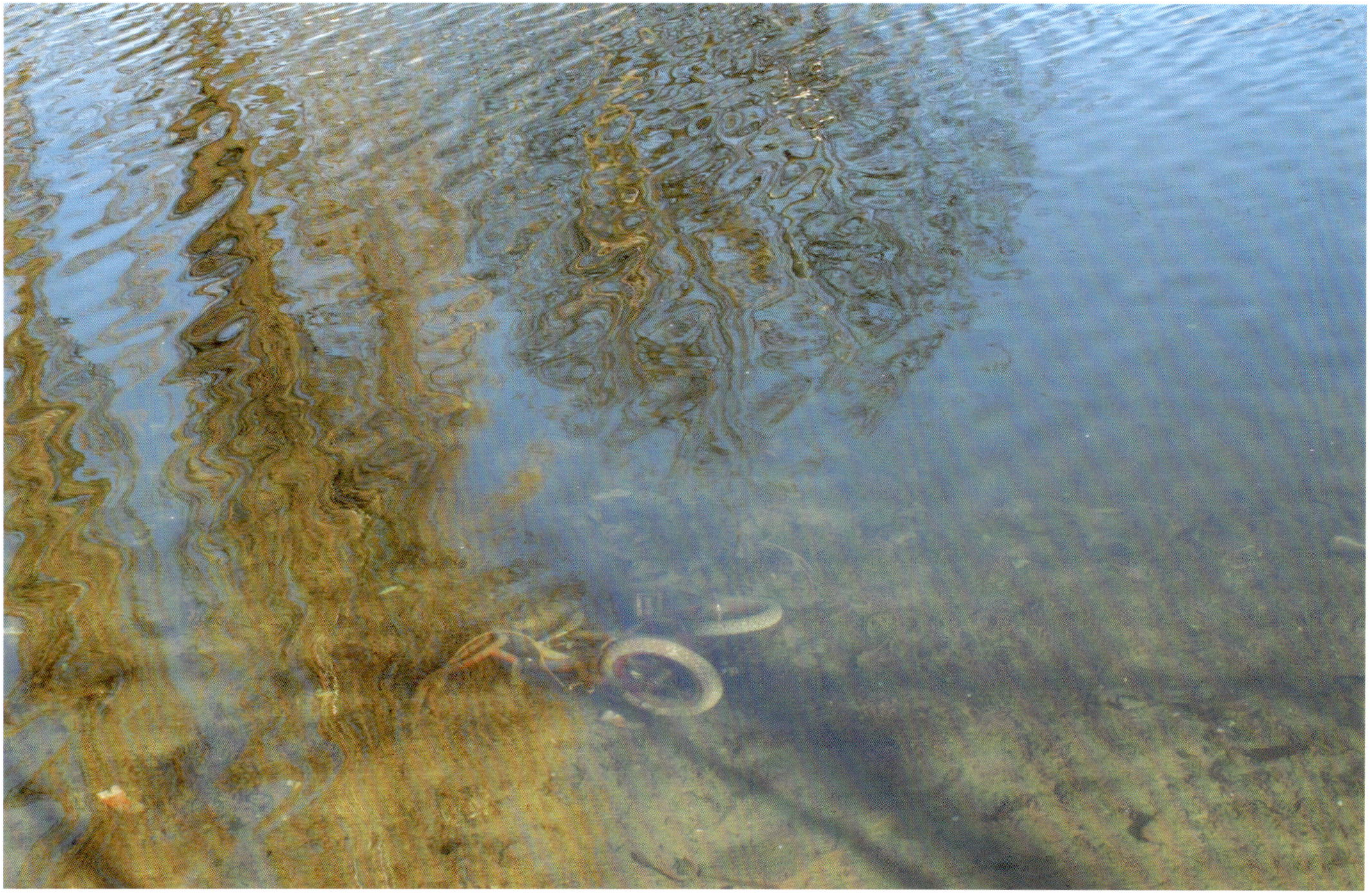

Man Walking on Monastery Road, Clondalkin, 2.15 a.m.

Dermot Bolger

You knew once what it felt like to truly be loved,
To belong absolutely with another presence:
A sense so intense you grew barely aware of it.

But now you sense it acutely by its absence,
By her indifference when you lie segregated
In the cold war zones of a partitioned mattress.

You know it's gone because you're stricken with panic,
Invisible, bereft of worth, feeling that you do no exist
Because you no longer see yourself reflected in her iris

Enlarged by love, held secure there, made complete.
You are two commuters now who fleetingly meet
On route to the bathroom or breakfast counter.

And tonight it feels like thirty years has dissolved,
Once again you're a youth adrift on neon-lit streets,
The young man who thought he was rescuing her,

The young man whom she rescued from loneliness,
The lost soul, exploring lanes, reluctant to turn home,
Resurrected inside the old man you've suddenly become.

Spy in the Sky

Mae Newman

As I sit unseen, I silently watch
Cars crawl and stop like carapaces.
Inside these shells people drink

Coffee, eat breakfast, shave,
Scratch, pluck eyebrows, use mobiles.
Ask the mirror –is this life?

They're too busy going somewhere,
Getting nowhere, to wonder
Am I lost, cast aside or rejected.

Some say I'm cute, I'm lovely.
Others that I'm cruel, I'm vermin.

A lonely grey squirrel, sitting
On a signpost over the bypass

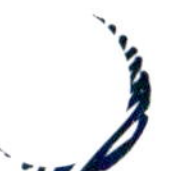

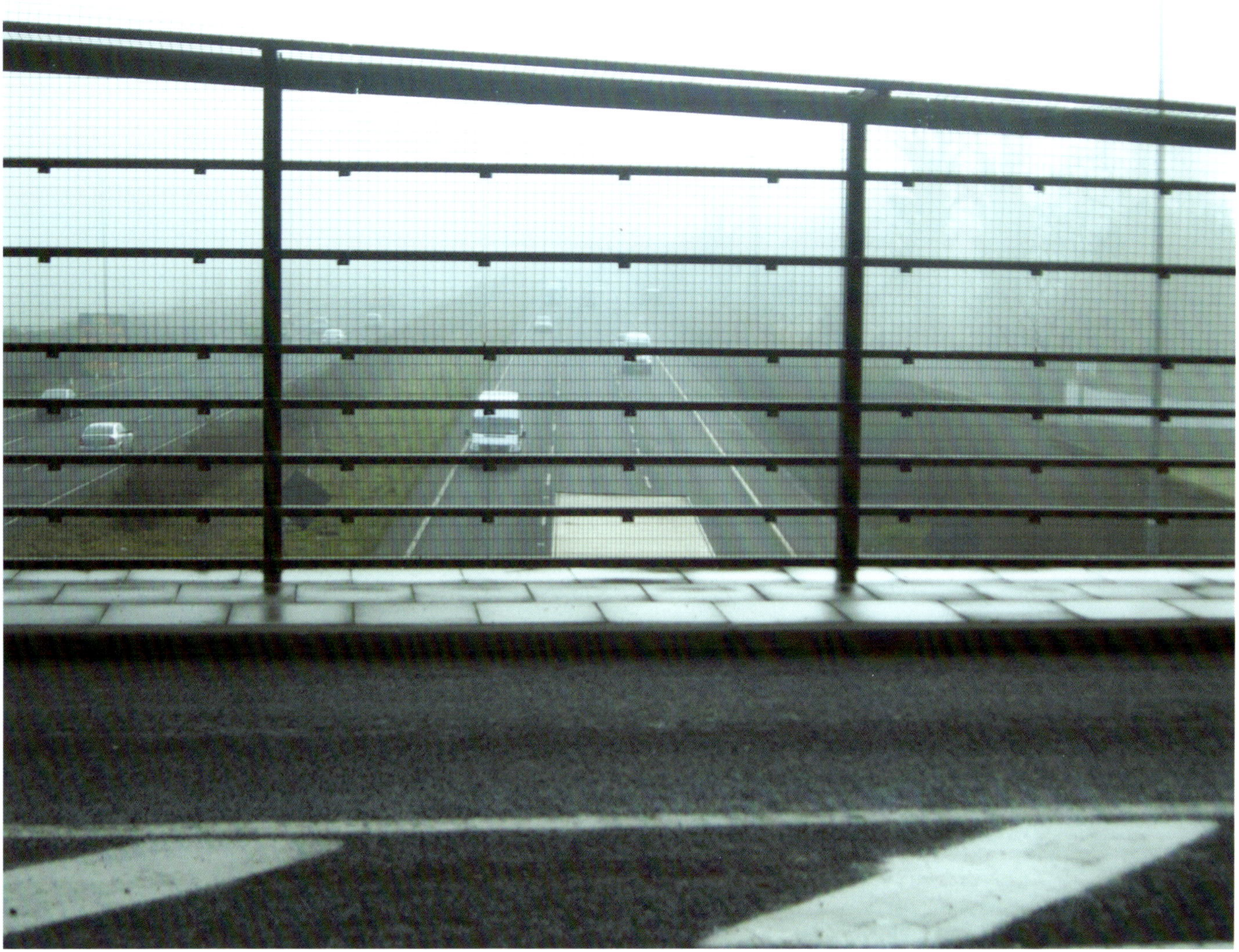

Jesus of Clondalkin

Dermot Bolger

Maybe Jesus is wandering these roads tonight,
Unrecognised, unacknowledged, utterly alone,

Passing half built apartment blocks investors own,
Passing burnt-out cars, glass shards, twisted chrome,

Threading a path through Neilstown and Quarryvale,
In Dunnes Stores white socks, with his jacket torn.

Maybe we are so adrift in our own cares that we fail
To see whip marks, collapsed veins, his crown of thorns.

Possibility

Dermot Bolger

Just leave yourself open to the possibility
That one dawn you wake to find your mind clear,

One dawn you win back the love you derailed,
One dawn you will kick the habit of blaming yourself.

One dawn you will wake to hear a clear signal,
A wavelength unmuffled by interference or static,

You will recognise the DJ's voice as your own
Advertising a unique extravaganza treasure hunt
Where each clue is a signpost through your past.

You will walk through a maze of sleeping estates,
Collecting golden tickets concealed amid mistakes
You made when addiction stopped you thinking straight.

That dawn, when figures emerge amidst the chaos,
You will walk forward, unafraid to embrace happiness.